Paolo Messa

THE AGE OF SHARP POWER

The influence of China, Russia and Iran abroad: the Italy case

Introduction by
Francesco Bechis

Typesetting: Laura Panigara, Cesano Boscone (MI)

Copyright © 2019 Bocconi University Press
EGEA S.p.A.

EGEA S.p.A.
Via Salasco, 5 - 20136 Milano
Tel. 02/5836.5751 – Fax 02/5836.5753
egea.edizioni@unibocconi.it – www.egeaeditore.it

All rights reserved, including but not limited to translation, total or partial adaptation, reproduction, and communication to the public by any means on any media (including microfilms, films, photocopies, electronic or digital media), as well as electronic information storage and retrieval systems. For more information or permission to use material from this text, see the website www.egeaeditore.it.

Given the characteristics of the Internet, the publisher is not responsible for any changes of address and content of the websites mentioned.

First edition: May 2019

ISBN Epub Italian Edition   978-88-99902-55-1
ISBN International Edition   978-88-85486-84-3
ISBN Epub International and Mobipocket Edition 978-88-85486-85-0

Table of Contents

Introduction, by *Francesco Bechis*		1
1	**Once Upon a Time, There was Soft Power**	7
	Soft power and public diplomacy	9
	Cultural exchange	10
	From manuals to constitutions	12
	Art and soft power	13
	Sports and soft power	15
	The media and soft power	16
	Soft power or propaganda?	18
	Notes	19
2	**Power Becomes Sharp**	21
	The link with authoritarian regimes	23
	The status of the debate	26
	The echo on the Old Continent	27
	An unprecedented threat	31
	Notes	32
3	**The ABCs of Sharp Power**	35
	Propaganda and sharp power	39
	"Telling a good story": the Chinese strategy	41
	Information or cyberwarfare? The Russian strategy	43
	Not only China and Russia: the Middle East	49
	Sharp cash: the Chinese New Silk Road	50
	Hitting the gas: the power of energy	53
	Notes	55

4	**Where the Battle is Fought, in Cyberspace**	59
	Cyberwarfare: nobody is safe	61
	The Russian Bear and cyber warfare: a successful marriage	63
	Glasses, coat and tie: the cyber face of the Dragon	68
	Iran: the last to arrive (not to be underestimated)	73
	Notes	77
5	**The Russian Bear's Tracks in Italy**	79
	From soft power ...	80
	... to sharp power	83
	(Successful) attempts at agenda setting	84
	Who funds online propaganda?	87
	From the web to the polls	90
	Linked, from the start	91
	If the trolls enter the action	95
	Notes	101
6	**China is Close, Very Close**	103
	The Dragon and the Boot	103
	When the claws come out ...	105
	Not just Confucius: the Italian-Chinese connection	106
	Italy is also present on the Silk Road	108
	The designs on strategic infrastructure	109
	Red, yellow, green: continuous links between Rome and Beijing	111
	Notes	113

Conclusions	115
Acknowledgments	121
Index of names	123

*to Lola and Nina,
so they remember that peace
is the result of a daily commitment*

Introduction

by *Francesco Bechis**

Has the world entered a second Cold War? It is hard to answer this question, which has vexed Western academics and political elites for some years now. Perhaps it is only fear, a worry to hide from ourselves because we do not want to re-open a chapter considered to be closed with the victory of the Western bloc. As the Harvard political scientist Stephen Walt wrote in *Foreign Policy*, reducing the new competition for power to an analogy with the past risks "laying the basis for a disastrous foreign policy."[1] There is something to Walt's argument. Indeed many of the most fascinating writings of the last century, whether intentionally or not, succumbed to reality, from the prophecy of the "end of history" by Francis Fukuyama, to the inevitable decline of the United States of America predicted in the writings of Paul Kennedy. Yet in reading the pages of this book it seems that the symptoms of a sort of second half of the Cold War are indeed present. Powers such as Russia, China and Iran are acting to demonstrate that their place in history and in the geography of the world is not at the margins of the United States of America. Moscow, despite an apparently more accommodating line from the Donald Trump Administration, is threatening the Americans on multiple fronts, from the Near Abroad (the territory that includes the former Soviet republics) to the Middle East. Beijing and Washington are in turn engaged in a military escalation in East Asia and in the South China Sea, as well as a no-holds-barred

---

* Born in 1995, master's student in Political Science at the Luiss University, author of comments and interviews for *Formiche.net*.
[1] S. Walt, "I knew the Cold War: This is no Cold War," *Foreign Policy*, 12/3/2018, www.foreignpolicy.com.

trade war. The United States must limit the regional hegemony of Iran in Lebanon, Syria, Iraq, Yemen and even Qatar. It is a hybrid war, very different than the one that for 40 years saw the Soviet bloc as a counter to the Atlantic bloc. The cybernetic revolution, as this book explains well, has radically changed the rules of the game, opening a new front in which it is difficult to distinguish lone wolves from the military units of their respective countries. Spies with coats, ties and briefcases have given way to much more effective cyber-espionage. The influence of television has been replaced by the penetration of *trolls* on the web and in social media.

The United States and Europe designed the system of multilateral institutions that guided international relations for 50 years, and continues to do so. They created the United Nations and also NATO, the largest and longest-lasting military alliance in history. They decided the rules of the international economy, imposing the dollar as the reference currency and laying the foundation for what would become the World Trade Organization. They at least won the battle, if not the war, of ideas in the twentieth century. To say it with Joseph Nye, Western *soft power* won in global media and culture. Today precisely this primacy is called strongly into question. The rediscovery of national identity and the search for geopolitical repositioning that does justice to a country's historical weight unites all of the countries that were defeated by, or surrendered to, the Cold War. This desire for *révanche* takes on very different forms depending on the state in question. Those who wish to reduce it to a simple Hobbesian struggle for power are wrong. Behind the rediscovery of identity of these peoples and the return of conflict with the West there are very solid cultural references and deep historical roots.

The heart of the Russian project of hegemony is in its leader: Vladimir Putin. A former KGB official stationed in Dresden, East Germany, Putin saw the collapse of the Soviet Union with his own eyes, from a European perspective; it is no surprise that he called it "the greatest geopolitical catastrophe of the twentieth century." The path outlined by the secretary of the Communist Party of the Soviet Union, Mikhail Gorbachev, based on *glasnost* and *perestroika* did not succeed in opening Russia to the rest of the world. The confused and dramatic transition entrusted to Boris Yeltsin aggravated the implosion of what remained of the old Soviet empire, and still today is an open wound in the collective memory of Russia. In this tragic interval of history, Putin's dream was born to transform Moscow into a Third Rome, a point of reference not only for the Slavic world but also for Eurasia. This is a mission that the Czar still feels today, and that dusts off the design of a great Eurasia from Ukraine to Manchuria, of a "land power" that counters a "sea power," to paraphrase Carl Schmitt. This design had already been endorsed in the 1990s by former Prime Minister Yevgeny Primakov, the teacher of the current Foreign Minister Sergey Lavrov and a great supporter of the Russian presence in the Middle East, and then structured in the thinking of the Eurasian movement of Alexander Dugin, an intellectual very close to the Russian president. Today this has become a specific foreign policy line, that is producing results. Putin's Russia has extended its sphere of influence in the former Soviet republics, finding in the Visegrad Group an ally that is increasingly aligned with the Kremlin. The invasion of Crimea in 2014 and the intervention in the Syrian civil war are additional pieces of a challenge to "Euro-Atlantic hegemony" – they are convinced of this in Moscow – that will have to be launched by a Great Russia able to fulfill its historical role as a superpower.

Unlike Russia, China and Iran share the wound of being past victims of Western colonialism. They are still today the spokesmen for the political legacy of the Conference of Bandung of 1955 and the non-aligned movement born in Berlin in 1961. It is sufficient to listen to a speech by Chinese President Xi Jinping to understand how vivid the wound of the "century of humiliation" is in Chinese historical memory: from the British domination of the nineteenth century to the Japanese invasion in the first half of the twentieth century (it was Xi Jinping who in 2014 proclaimed a national day of mourning for the Nanking Massacre of 1937).

The aspirations of these two nations are very different. The Chinese shift is linked to Xi's rise to the top of the Communist Party. A child of a revolutionary, and currently party secretary and president of the republic indefinitely, Xi climbed the ladder of power with the solemn promise to renew the "Chinese dream": a China that is a protagonist on a global level, reunited with its communities around the world, prosperous and hegemonic on an economic and military level. It is a *fil rouge* that in recent years has accompanied "Xi's Thought," now enshrined in the Constitution, an honor that in the past was reserved only for Mao and Deng. The global scope of the influence of Xi, the former governor of Fujian, has three aspects. The first is cultural. Since he took over as party secretary, Xi has definitively ended the era of technocrats from the Deng Xiaoping era, returning the most dangerous type of people to the Forbidden City: philosophers. Thus, without touching the thought of Mao and Karl Marx,

China has rediscovered its ancient wise men, starting with Confucius, who for years was banned by the Communist Party. The recovery of tradition has gone hand in hand with a strategy of cultural influence abroad to contrast the Western monopoly. The immense network of the Confucius Institutes, the cultural centers inaugurated by Hu Jintao and considerably strengthened under Xi's presidency, is the most evident example of this new global Chinese effort. The second aspect is political. At home, together with a strong grasp on the party cadres and on propaganda, Xi has imposed a personality cult similar to the one centered on Mao; so much for those who thought that globalization in China would proceed hand in hand with political liberalization. On the foreign front, Xi's China is challenging the American presence in Asia and Oceania, although never seeking a direct confrontation, and has almost eliminated the European presence in the Eastern portion of Africa. Lastly, is economics: the goal is to inaugurate an alternative model to American capitalism through the construction of new multilateral institutions such as the Asian Infrastructure Investment Bank and direct investment in foreign countries. The greatest challenge to the world economic order today comes from the colossal One Belt One Road project, the New Silk Road by which Beijing wishes to unite Europe, Asia and Africa by sea and land.

The Iran of Hassan Rouhani and Ayatollah Ali Khamenei is an assertive player in foreign policies that sees the United States as a sworn enemy. In his messages to the nation, the supreme leader Khamenei frequently defines the United States as the "Great Satan." Rouhani's election as president in 2013, despite bringing with it a hope for changes in foreign policy, did not mark a significant break with the tragic political legacy left by Mahmoud Ahmadinejad. The former president, who left Rouhani a country that was isolated and buckling under international sanctions, may have been banned by the political elites of Teheran. However, his foreign policy has not undergone great changes. The nuclear agreement signed in 2015 with Europe and the United States of Barack Obama (Joint Comprehensive Plan of Action) raised hopes for a new era in relations between Iran and the West. When US President Donald Trump decided to withdraw from the agreement, many, starting with the European countries that had worked hard on the deal, including Italy, accused the White House of destabilizing the Middle East. Yet there is no doubt that the Rouhani regime has continued to sponsor an aggressive foreign policy towards the United States and its allies, especially towards the sworn enemies of the Islamic Republic: Saudi Arabia and Israel. On the other hand, Teheran has succeeded in weaving a diplomatic web that has brought the country closer to both Putin's Russia and Xi's China. The strategy was summarized in the words pronounced by Khamenei during a visit to Azerbaijan at the start of 2018: "In foreign policy, the top priorities for us today include preferring East to West, preferring neighboring countries to far reached locations."

It is not easy to pinpoint the start of this second phase of the Cold War. Historians have long debated what reference point to take for the onset of the first. The Yalta Conference? The Greek Civil War? The Soviet coup in Czechoslovakia in 1948? There is no single answer. The analysis by Paolo Messa seems to favor the period of 2013-14 as the moment of a strategic break that marks the start of a new season in international relations. March 2013: Xi Jinping becomes president of the People's Republic of China. August 2013: Hassan Rouhani wins the elections and becomes president of the Islamic Republic of Iran. March 2014: the "little green men" sent by Moscow invade Crimea. In those 12 months we find the seeds of a resumption of conflicts in the international field, although no longer between only two powers. The clash is based on variable geometries, that does involve the use of military force, but also that of new instruments: information warfare, investments in strategic infrastructure of third countries, and a new battle for cultural hegemony. And above all, cybernetic warfare, to which this book dedicates an entire chapter.

Great changes in history require a rethinking of the categories with which we have learned to read events. The narration of soft power as a method of interpretation of international relations so brilliantly launched by Joseph Nye at the beginning of the nineties succeeded in going mainstream. It entered think tanks, universities and even the constitutions and programmatic documents of some states. But is it really still sufficient, alone, to interpret the struggle for hegemony that characterizes this century? This is the question this book aims to answer, without claiming to be exhaustive. It throws light on a new form of power that seems sharper, quieter and more dangerous, suited to explain the new challenge from China, Russia and Iran to the West: *sharp power*. The expression was first used in November 2017 in a report by the National Endowment for Democracy (NED), a well-known American think tank founded by Ronald Reagan. As we will see, the NED researchers denounced the attempt by China and Russia to penetrate the political systems of democratic countries with a new cultural offensive that takes on the guise of unscrupulous political propaganda.

The study has provoked ferocious criticism and a lively academic debate, in which this book aims to intervene, broadening the field of study to other, more intrusive forms of influence in the internal affairs of a state. Investments in critical infrastructure, the use of trolls and bots to spread propaganda and fake news on the web; and then cyberwarfare, the inevitable conclusion of the cyber revolution of the twenty-first century, a reality that involves efforts by both democratic states and illiberal regimes. Finally, the book offers an exceptional panorama of the network of Russian and Chinese influence in Italy. The Eurasian states seek to use Italy as a door to enter the West. We must be conscious of this goal, to avoid gifting foreign powers easy access to western political system and strategic national assets.

1 Once Upon a Time, There was Soft Power

Let us imagine that a parent has only two options to prevent a child from using vulgar language: the first is to strike him and lock him in the house every time he pronounces a bad word, and the second is to give a good example, raising the child to be accustomed to polite and even-tempered language. If the parent chooses the first option, he will probably obtain the opposite of what he wishes. The conclusion is intuitive, and almost banal. Yet that was sufficient for one of the greatest current American political analysts, Professor Emeritus Joseph Nye of Harvard, to find a key for interpreting international relations that has taken its place in university manuals around the world: soft power. Why use force when you can obtain more, and at a lower cost, with ideas? Following the abundant literature produced by Nye on the issue, we can define soft power as the ability to obtain something through attraction rather than coercion. Let us go into detail: transposed into the world of inter-state relations, the soft power of a state consists of its ability to persuade other states to join a system of rules and institutions suited to one's own interests, and recognize their legitimacy.

"This second aspect of power – which occurs when one country gets other countries to want what it wants – might be called co-optive or soft power in contrast with the hard or command power of ordering others to do what it wants" Nye explained in *Bound to Lead*, a book that has become a benchmark in the field.[1] It was 1990, the Berlin Wall was reduced to rubble, and what little was left intact was being demolished by Mikhail Gorbachev through *glasnost* and *perestroika*. The end of the Cold War was giving rise to the myth of a new unipolar era in which the United States would no longer have any rivals, contradicting the arguments of those who had predicted the inexorable decline of America, with great success in bookstores at the end of the eighties, thanks to pages written by respected analysts such as Paul Kennedy, David Calleo and Oswald Spengler.[2] Almost 30 years later, Nye's book is still relevant today, and is widely cited in political debate. So it is appropriate to follow his treatment of the matter to examine soft power, a word that is as appreciated in the academic world as it is abused in foreign policy circles.

Soft power is certainly not a new tool in international relations. Supremacy in armed conflict and military tactics allowed Alexander the Great to defeat the Persia of the great King Darius III, to subdue Syria, Phoenicia and Mesopotamia. Yet the fascinating nature of Persian culture, which infatuated him to the point that he instituted a cult of personality and imposed genuflection even on his most trusted men, set the Macedonian troops against him and marked the beginning of his downfall. History is full of similar examples. The resources invested by the French monarchs of the seventeenth and eighteenth centuries in the promotion of their culture abroad triggered a race to *grandeur* among the other European states. French become the language of European diplomacy, to the point that it was spoken fluently in the courts of Prussia and Russia. A similar competition occurred with the advent of radio and movies in the twentieth century. The birth of the BBC in 1922 allowed the United Kingdom to enter the houses of millions of people in just a few years. Even dictatorial regimes such as Italy in the 20 years of Fascism and national-socialist Germany sponsored broadcasts in English to spread their propaganda abroad. Today states do just as much to use culture, tradition and their national reputation to seek consensus abroad and gain legitimacy in the eyes of the international community. Not only do states have their own specific soft power; businesses, non-governmental organizations and even celebrities can exert influence that is much deeper and more decisive than a state. Without a long negotiating process carried out by the Sant'Egidio Community, a Catholic movement born in 1968, Mozambique would not have emerged from 17 years of civil war. On October 4, 1992, Mozambique President Joaquim Chissano and the leader of the independence faction Afonso Dhlakama signed an historic peace agreement at the Sant'Egidio Community offices in Rome, not at the Ministry of Foreign Affairs, or in some other embassy. Culture, tradition and collective imagination constitute the basis for the soft power of a state. If the Marshall Plan had been limited to providing humanitarian and financial aid to Europe in the post-war period, the legacy of the United States probably would have been cut short, and would not have been sufficient to slow the advance of the Iron Curtain. The success of the plan went well beyond the 2 percent of GDP spent in supplies; the aid succeeded in creating a sense of gratitude and admiration in European countries towards their American ally, but the films of Hollywood, Coca-Cola and Virginia tobacco also played a role.

Soft power and public diplomacy

There are different ways the culture of a country contributes to its soft power. A first instrument is public diplomacy.

Technological progress and the evolution of the web have profoundly transformed the diplomatic world. Today the credibility of a state, and the health of its public image abroad, is just as important in international relations as other levers such as economic and military power.

Culture plays a leading role in the construction of soft power, but is not sufficient by itself. Soft power is not only passive attraction or persuasion, it is mutual interaction. Without fertile ground it cannot take root and have an effect on the recipient. To use Nye's words, soft power is a "couple dance."[3] An important bilateral meeting between two heads of state or government risks falling apart, or not producing the desired results, if proper attention is not given to the smallest details. Soft power can shift the balance and determine the success or failure of negotiations. When in November 2010 former British Prime Minister David Cameron went on an official visit to Beijing with a delegation of ministers and a large group of businessmen to discuss trade agreements, he was the victim of a misunderstanding covered on the front pages of international tabloids in the following days. All of the representatives of the English government who were present, including Cameron, were proudly wearing a red poppy flower on their lapels, a common symbol throughout the Commonwealth to commemorate Remembrance Day, November 11, a day dedicated to the fallen in war. The British ministers were speechless when Chinese officials asked them to remove the flower from their jackets. In China the poppy flower evokes a painful chapter of history, the humiliating defeat in the two Opium Wars (1839–42; 1856–60), fought against the British Empire; opium is the substance obtained from that red flower. The firm refusal by the British ministers of their hosts' request risked ruining the institutional visit and undermining British soft power in China.

Sometimes soft power can facilitate a meeting between two heads of state or government who have distant, or even opposite, ideological positions. On July 14, 2017, US President Donald Trump, on an official visit to Paris, watched the traditional military parade to commemorate the Storming of the Bastille and 100 years since the US intervention in the First World War, next to French President Emmanuel Macron. The succession of tanks, jets and military bands through the streets of the capital so impressed Trump that he promised to replicate the performance for the July 4 holiday in the States. It became a true obsession for the American president: once he returned home, he immediately directed his allies on Capitol Hill to organize a parade in grand style on Pennsylvania Avenue. Trump and Macron have often found themselves holding opposite positions: for example on the Paris Climate Agreement (Cop21), the Iran Nuclear Agreement, and support for the European Union. Yet the triumphal march on the Champs-Elysées marked the start of a visible improvement in bilateral relations, that culminated with Macron's state visit to Washington in April 2018, when he and his wife participated in a sumptuous state dinner at the White House. Two days after the departure of the French president, Trump received German Chancellor Angela Merkel, holding a closed-door meeting of a few hours and a chilly press conference. Soft power emerges also, and above all, in the details.

Cultural exchange

A second instrument which nation-states use to increase their soft power abroad is cultural exchange. Investing in student exchange programs and partnerships with universities abroad can be a successful strategy to increase influence. During the Cold War, the cultural exchanges in which the children of Russian elites participated to study at prestigious US universities played a leading role in the spread of American ideas and culture behind the Iron Curtain, starting a slow, gradual process of liberalization in the Soviet Union. According to one study, those programs can even be considered as the starting point for the decline of the USSR.[4] Oleg Kalugin, a former KGB general, who between 1958 and 1959 studied at Columbia University, confirmed the impact of cultural exchanges abroad on the power structure of the USSR: "Exchanges were a Trojan Horse in the Soviet Union. They played a tremendous role in the erosion of the Soviet system. They opened up a closed society. They greatly influenced younger people who saw the world with more open eyes, and they kept infecting more and more people over the years."[5]

Today one of the countries that invests the most in cultural exchange programs is China. If the Dragon has succeeded in changing its face abroad in the past 20 years, this is due also to the exceptional flow of students who have abandoned their mother country to study in Asia, Europe and America. The United States is the preferred destination. Chinese students represent the largest group of foreign students enrolled in American universities. According to a report of the Institute of International Education, in 2016–17 the number of Chinese students studying at US colleges was 350,755, approximately 35 percent of all foreign students.[6] The statistics published by the Chinese government show that in 2017 alone, 480,900 Chinese citizens who studied abroad returned to China to look for work.[7] So in most cases, it is not a one-way trip. Once they have received an undergraduate or master's degree, the students return to China to place the know-how and skills obtained at the service of their country. This is a phenomenon not limited to the upper middle class; it reaches into the highest levels of politics. The anti-American rhetoric of some leading representatives of the Communist Party of China (CPC) clashes with a trend that has been strengthened over the years: many of the old and new party leaders, including some members of the Politburo, have children who study abroad, almost always in US universities. Even the daughter of Chinese president Xi Jinping, Xi Mingze, enrolled in Harvard in 2010 under a pseudonym, to then graduate four years later. The experience of studying abroad usually leaves a positive impression in the Chinese students and helps grow American soft power in China once they return. Already at the end of the nineties, in an interview with *Newsweek*, the son of former Chinese Foreign Minister Qian Qichen, who had studied at the University of Michigan, explained the effect of cultural exchanges between the two sides of the ocean: "Our experiences made us see that there are alternative ways for China to develop and for us to lead our personal lives. Being in the United States made us realize that things in China can be different."[8]

From manuals to constitutions

For some time now, soft power has abandoned the cramped walls of the academic world and think tanks to enter the common language of international policy. Today there is even an index, the *Soft Power 30*, published by Portland Communications and the Center on Public Diplomacy of the University of Southern California that presents a list of the top 30 countries in the world in terms of the exercise of soft power. The scientific nature of the criteria adopted is undoubtedly difficult to verify, yet every year newspapers dedicate considerable space to the listing. The term coined by Nye is also used increasingly frequently in the institutions. In 2018, for example, the British government published a national security capability review where it proposed to "create a cross-government soft power strategy," because "how the UK is perceived matters."[9]

The phenomenon is not limited to Western diplomacy. In 2013, the Russian Foreign Minister had already included soft power in an official document as among the priorities of the Kremlin's foreign policy, defining it as "an indispensable component of international relations."[10] In the Middle East as well, some countries led by conservative religious elites are attempting to change course to improve their image abroad. This is so in the United Arab Emirates, for example, that on request from Prime Minister Mohammed Bin Rashid Al Maktoum even established a "UAE Soft Power Council" in April 2017, a body that responds directly to the government. In September of that same year, the Center published a "soft power strategy" aimed at "increasing the country's global reputation abroad."[11] The most evident case remains that of China, though. For years the leaders of the Communist Party of China, including former President Hu Jintao and the current inhabitant of the Forbidden City Xi Jinping, have explicitly cited soft power as a useful resource to seal China's place among world powers. Yet the expression had never been formalized in a constitutional document. This happened in 2017, when at the 19th Congress of the CPC, the expression soft power, born and grown in an American university, was entered and immortalized in the constitution of the party that governs a country of almost 2 billion people. The text reads: "The Party will work to develop educational, scientific and cultural initiatives, promote creative evolution and innovative development of traditional Chinese culture, bring forward our revolutionary culture, develop an advanced socialist culture and improve our country's cultural soft power." A term coined by an American political scientist from Harvard is now written in black and white in the document of the single party in China, and will be studied by Chinese students, from elementary school to university. Nye himself highlighted the responsibility, with a provocation launched on Twitter: "So now 'soft power' is written into the constitution of Chinese party. Wonder how Xi will use it?"

Art and soft power

We see that the concept of soft power does not attract the attention only of political analysts and the press. Governments construct ad hoc policies and commit entire categories of expenditures to promoting soft power. Investing public resources in art, music and literature can be an important means for gaining consent and credibility in the eyes of the international community. This is even truer for those states that wish to set aside a murky past, rediscover old alliances or start new ones. Obviously, art can be an instrument of hard power or pure propaganda. Consider the case of museums: in a not-too-distant past absolute monarchies or nation-states created museums to preserve (and rewrite) the history of their countries, to celebrate military conquests and give evidence of victory over the "enemy." Today museums are mostly managed by non-profit entities or independent administrations. In the United States, over 80 percent of museums are controlled by independent organizations. The trend is global: everywhere we see shifts from the state to civil society and very varied forms of financing. This is because states, even when they have an authoritarian government, have realized the strategic importance of independent museums to promote national soft power: they preserve the past, but at the same time they give a vivid image of the health of the country and attract minds, visitors and investment from abroad.

The construction of a successful museum can change the face of a city, relaunch its economy and become an emblem of the city itself. When about 20 years ago the Canadian architect Frank Gehry was hired for the construction of the Guggenheim museum of Bilbao, the city was going through a serious identity crisis: annual visitors were less than 100,000, and tourism was disappearing in part due to the shadow cast on the capital by years of Basque terrorism. Today the museum by itself has over 1 million visitors a year, and in the meantime hundreds of restaurants, hotels and shops have sprung up, making the city an enclave of Spanish soft power. The extraordinary success of the project gave the name to the "Bilbao effect": investments in culture and architectural works with a strong visual impact are the perfect recipe to revive cities that seem to be in decay.[12] The Ordos Museum in Kangbashi, in the heart of Mongolia, the Centre Pompidou in the small French city of Metz, and the Niemeyer Center in Avilés, a little Spanish town in the Asturias, are further examples of magnificent museum architecture designed to revive isolated or unattractive areas.

Gulf countries such as Qatar and the United Arab Emirates have learned the lesson. In this case, though, the *longa manus* of the government in the management of the museums is more evident compared to the situation in European countries. Since the late 2000s, these countries have launched some gigantic projects in the visual arts field, funded by the state. The dubious economic rationale behind some of these works reveals their true goal: not only to create profits, but above all to impress the international community, giving the image of an open, multicultural country, if possible dampening criticism from non-governmental organizations such as Human Rights Watch and Amnesty International regarding the violation of human rights and restrictions on freedom of expression through severe censure of media and social networks. The construction of works such as the Guggenheim Museum and the Louvre Abu Dhabi, funded by the Emirati public Tourism Development and Investment Company (TDIC), with delays and budget problems, was not so much aimed at expanding international tourism, but rather at satisfying the desire of the elites in power in the United Arab Emirates to export their country's brand abroad. The inauguration of the Louvre Abu Dhabi ended up being a success for French President Emmanuel Macron as well, who decided to be present at the opening ceremony. The finalization of the agreement turned into a great deal for the famous Paris museum, that received 525 million dollars for a 30 year rental of the brand, and another 750 million, divided among affiliated museums, for the works of art and personnel lent to the Emirates. In his speech at the opening of the museum, Macron stressed the strategic importance of the Louvre Abu Dhabi to improve bilateral relations through French soft power: "Try us, please! Not only our wine or luxury items, but also our culture and the universal and humanitarian values reflected in it."[13]

A similar example can be seen in the case of the Islamic Art Museum in Doha, Qatar. Despite the name, the museum was built in 2008 under the supervision of the Qatar Museums Authority (QM), a state entity led by Princess Al Mayassa Al Thani, for an exclusively international audience. The exhibition of Greek nudes repeatedly aroused indignation in the local community, that mobilized to the point of forcing the Qatari authorities to intervene and cover some of the statues. Similar protests occurred at other events organized under the sponsorship of the QM, such as the Doha Tribeca Film Festival and the installation of sculptures by international artists.[14]

Sports and soft power

If music and visual arts are a powerful instrument in the hands of a state to promote its soft power, sports can also play a role. By now there is a wealth of literature on so-called sport diplomacy: large sports events are precious occasions to expand knowledge of a country's culture, traditions, values and economic prosperity abroad.

Sometimes, like culture, sports can be used by states as a tool of propaganda and hard power. In the thirties the Fascists in Italy and the National-socialists in Germany made sports events their preferred channel to show off their military and economic power. It is not rare in history for large sports events to be the target of terrorist attacks, or the venue for diplomatic clashes, boycotts or other forms of protest. In most cases, though, governments decide to invest in these types of events to improve their image and make new allies.

There are various ways to conduct diplomacy through sports.[15] The first is to invest large amounts of money in a sport which attracts great media attention, purchasing clubs and launching targeted media campaigns. This is what is happening in soccer, where countries such as Qatar and China are rapidly rising in the ranks of the states that spend the most in the sport.[16] The purchase of the Paris Saint Germain club by Qatar Sports Investments, a branch of the Qatar Investment Authority, in 2012, the sponsorship of a team like Barcelona by the Qatar Foundation, and the arrival in the Qatari league of the star Xavi, have proven to be profitable investments in terms of public image.

A second option is to host global events such as the soccer World Cup or the Olympic Games. Germany may not have won the FIFA World Cup in Berlin in 2006, but it still came out on top: impeccable organization, record numbers for proceeds and visitors, and a festive environment that was defined as a "summer fairy tale" revived Germany's image in the world, substituting the rhetoric of a country dominating Europe with that of a friendly, open and multicultural nation. During a public event a few months afterwards, Chancellor Merkel herself stated: "The world met a new Germany."[17] Likewise, the 2008 Olympics in Beijing were conceived by the Chinese government to be a driver of the Dragon's soft power in the world. Just a few months earlier, on October 15, 2007, during the 17th Congress of the CPC, President Hu Jintao had formally inaugurated China's new grand strategy: "enhance culture as part of soft power of our country to better guarantee the people's basic cultural rights and interests." The firework displays of the opening ceremony, the extraordinary success of Chinese athletes, and the media impact of stars like basketball player Yao Ming hit the mark, but only partially.[18] The view of the Olympic Games in Beijing did not hide the country's problems from the international press: state management of sports, censure of media and political opponents, pollution of Chinese cities and the March 2008 repression of the Tibetan revolt in the city of Lhasa drew harsh criticism from the Western world, balancing out, and possibly even entirely cancelling, the positive effect the Olympics had on Beijing's soft power.

Organizing a global sports event entails some risks. Qatar is currently experiencing this, as it prepares to host the soccer World Cup in 2022. It is an historical opportunity for Doha, that is still paying the price of isolation due to accusations of terrorist financing by Gulf countries and the United States. The security conditions in which a million and a half migrants are forced to work to build the stadiums, without passports or visas to leave the country, along with the suspicions raised by the investigations conducted by Swiss and US authorities on the way Qatar won the vote in 2010 to host the Cup, risk further undermining Qatari soft power, frustrating the government's enormous financial effort.

The media and soft power

Information remains the most powerful instrument to export culture, values and ideas abroad, and to win over public opinion. Broadcast networks such as BBC, CNN and Al Jazeera that are available 24 hours a day outside of national borders, and in multiple languages, have a fundamental role in the construction of the public images of their respective countries. During the Cold War the United States invested considerable public resources to fund Voice of America (VOA), the federal radio and television service that still today broadcasts in over 40 languages. Alongside radio broadcasters such as Radio Liberty and Radio Free Europe, VOA proved to be an effective weapon to spread US culture and ideas behind the Iron Curtain, where it inaugurated the first transmission on February 17, 1947 with a now celebrated sentence: "Hello! This is New York calling." Over the years, however, there was harsh criticism even from American public opinion about the way these broadcasts were managed, being controlled by the government.

The dividing line between the promotion of culture and propaganda can become thin when speaking of such large subjects as public information channels. China Central Television (CCTV) was born in 1978 to be the official voice of the CPC. Today it is a global network, broadcasting content in Mandarin, Russia, English, Arabic, Spanish and French. It has 50 channels, headquarters in Beijing, Nairobi and Washington, and over a billion users. Together with the two other leading broadcasters in China, China National Radio and China Radio International, it answers directly to the Propaganda headquarters. State censure of Chinese media, however, does not always represent an obstacle to circulation abroad. The popularity of the Dragon's broadcast channels in the African continent, for example, increases every year. In 2012 the state television network CCTV opened a CCTV Africa channel, which today has a certain influence on the information provided by leading African newspapers. CCTV chose Kenya for the construction of one of its headquarters, *China Daily* has an African edition, as does StarTimes, a Beijing press agency mostly unknown in the West, but well-known to millions of Kenyans, Congolese and Central Africans. There are no doubts that Beijing's massive investments in the media system of Central and Western African countries have borne fruit. According to a survey conducted by Afrobarometer, 63 percent of Africans consider Chinese influence "fairly or very positive," with peaks reached in Mali (92 percent), Niger (84 percent) and Liberia (81 percent). In Central Africa positive public sentiment towards China among the citizens surveyed was even higher than towards the United States (35 percent versus 27 percent). The data is stunning, and demonstrates that soft power does not depend only on the sender, but also the recipient.

Another interesting case of how the media can change the public image of a country is that of Al Jazeera. The very popular channel founded in Qatar in 1996 broadcasts in Arabic and English in more than 100 countries for a total of 300 million users, numbers which put it on the same level as media giants such as CNN and BBC. It has offices in Doha, Washington, London and Kuala Lumpur. Founded on request from the Emir Hamad bin Khalifa Al Thani with the goal of breaking the Saudi monopoly on Arabic information, Al Jazeera still represents one of Qatar's secret weapons today. The channel became famous abroad for a more lively approach to news, and less invasive censure than the mainstream media in the Gulf. It became a true eyesore for the Saudis, who in 2003 responded by blessing the birth of the Emirati broadcaster Al Arabiya, and in the summer of 2017, in the middle of the diplomatic crisis between Qatar and the Gulf countries, demanded that the Qatari station be closed as a condition for loosening the embargo. Although the direct financial and political connection linking the channel to the Al Thani royal family is evident, Al Jazeera remains a fully successful experiment that has reached the level of its Western competition. Its popularity in the Middle East and North Africa allows Qatar, a country with less than 3 million inhabitants and a territory similar to that of Connecticut, to make its voice heard at a level that greatly exceeds its actual weight in the international scenario.

Soft power or propaganda?

We have seen how soft power remains a valid instrument for interpreting international relations. Governments project policy with the aim of improving their image abroad, some even speaking of soft power in legislative and constitutional texts. In this chapter we have mentioned only some of the practical applications of soft power: diplomacy, direct cultural contacts, art, sports and mainstream media. There are many others. Film, peacekeeping missions and institutes for teaching foreign languages abroad are just as effective. It is important, though, not to overestimate the influence of soft power. The investment of financial resources in a policy for soft power risks being in vain if the target is not receptive, i.e. if fertile ground is lacking to accept the cultural and political model of a foreign country. China is able to exercise its soft power in Central and Western Africa, but cannot claim the same grip on its most unwieldy neighbor in Asia: India. Bilateral relations between the two regional powers, although they share 2,000 years of history, continue to be dictated by ancient mistrust.[19] A 2016 survey by the Pew Research Center shows that only 26 percent of Chinese have a positive opinion of Indians,[20] and another institute estimates that only 31 percent of Indians have a high regard for the Dragon.[21] The strongly stereotyped image that the Chinese media give of Indian society, underlining the iniquity of the caste system and the exploitation of women, certainly does not help reduce tensions.

Another error that can be committed is to consider soft power as a normative concept. There is nothing intrinsically positive or negative in soft power. Like military and economic power, it is an instrument that can be used for multiple purposes. As Joseph Nye recently stressed in *Foreign Affairs*, "it is not necessarily better to twist minds than twist arms."[22] This is exactly where the limit of the rich literature on soft power lies, that has filled the manuals of international relations in the last 30 years. How do we distinguish it from propaganda? Theoretically, Nye's definition of soft power can also apply to propaganda: is it not also "the ability to obtain something through attraction"? The so-called "lone wolves" who in recent years took part in terrorist attacks in Europe in the name of *jihad* did not do so for money, or through coercion. They did it because the jihadist message channeled through the web found fertile ground (social resentment, mental instability, personal experiences), and persuaded them to act. The positive meaning that has too often accompanied the concept of soft power in recent years has led to underestimating the harm that ruthless use of cultural influence can cause. In a world where the paradigm of competition between great powers is replacing global multilateralism, soft power is no longer sufficient to explain the relations between states in the international arena. A new form of power, much less *soft* and much more *sharp*, penetrating and silent, allows some states to extend their influence abroad. The levers are the same as soft power: culture, investments and diplomacy. But the *modus operandi* is entirely different.

Note

[1] J.S. Nye Jr, *Bound to Lead: The Changing Nature of American Power*, New York, Basic Books, 2016 (1st ed. 1990).
[2] D.P. Calleo, *Beyond American Hegemony: The Future of the Western Alliance*, New York, Basic Books, 1987; P. Kennedy, *The Rise and Fall of the Great Powers*, New York, Vintage, 2010; O. Spengler, *The Decline of the West*, Oxford, Oxford Paperbacks, 1991.

³ J.S. Nye Jr, "Get smart: Combining hard and soft power," *Foreign Affairs*, 88(4), 2009, pp. 160–163.

⁴ Y. Richmond, *Cultural Exchange and the Cold War: Raising the Iron Curtain*, Penn State Press, 2010.

⁵· *Ibid.*, p. 32.

⁶ Institute of International Eucation, *Open Doors 2017*, www.iie.org.

⁷ Ministry of Education of the People's Republic of China, "2017 sees increase in number of Chinese students studying abroad and returning after overseas studies," 4/4/2018, en.moe.gov.cn.

⁸ C. Atkinson, "Does soft power matter? A comparative analysis of student exchange programs 1980–2006," *Foreign Policy Analysis*, 6(1), 2010, pp. 1–22.

⁹ HM Government, *National Security Capability Review*, March 2018, assets.publishing.service.gov.uk.

¹⁰ The Ministry of Foreign Affairs of the Russian Federation, *Concept of the Foreign Policy of the Russian Federation*, 18/2/2013, http://www. mid.ru.

¹¹ *The UAE Soft Power Strategy*, government.ae, updated 26/4/2018.

¹² Portland, USC Center on Public Diplomacy, *The Soft Power 30. A Global Ranking of Soft Power*, 2017, Foreign Policy, softpower30.com.

¹³ R. Zaretsky, "The Louvre isn't just a museum. It's a power tool", *Foreign Policy*, 10/11/2017, foreignpolicy.com.

¹⁴ S. Hertog, *A Quest for Significance: Gulf Oil Monarchies' International "Soft Power" Strategies and their Local Urban Dimensions*, LSE Kuwait Programme Paper Series, n. 42, March 2017, eprints.lse.ac.uk.

¹⁵ E. Alberts, "The mixed records of sport diplomacy. Interview with Jonathan Grix," Council on Foreign Relations, 6/2/2018, www.cfr.org.

¹⁶ C. Murray, "Which countries spent the most money on transfers in 2016?," *Fox Sports*, 27/1/2017, www.foxsports.com.

¹⁷ "Germany celebrates a summer to remember," *Spiegel Online*, 4/10/2006, www.spiegel.de.

¹⁸ P. Zhongying, "The Beijing Olympics and China's soft power," Brookings, 4/9/2008, www.brookings.edu.

¹⁹ A. Qin, "China fears India may be edging it out in cultural battle," *New York Times*, 30/9/2017, www.nytimes.com.

²⁰ R. Wike, B. Stokes, "China and the world," Pew Research Center, 5/10/2016, www.pewglobal.org.

²¹ B. Stokes, "How Indians see their place in the world," Pew Research Center, 19/9/2016, www.pewglobal.org.

²² J.S. Nye Jr, "How sharp power threatens soft power," *Foreign Affairs*, 24/1/2018, www.foreignaffairs.com.

2   Power Becomes Sharp

In the summer of 2009, the University of North Carolina cancelled the meeting with the Dalai Lama Tenzin Gyatso, the Noble Peace Price winner and spiritual leader of Tibetan Buddhism, considered a traitor by the People's Republic of China. Bailian Li, local director of the Confucius Institute, the Chinese language institute hosted by thousands of universities in the world, asked the rector of the university Warwick Arden to go back on the commitment, because the Dalai Lama's speech would have been a risk for "the strong relations we are developing with China."[1] Arden himself then put an end to the controversy, admitting to *Bloomberg*: "I don't want to say we didn't think about whether there were implications. Of course you do. China is a major trading partner for North Carolina."[2] In the following years, many similar cases occurred. The Dalai Lama received more than one last-minute refusal from the universities that invited him to speak. Most of them host a Confucius Institute. That same year, the University of Tasmania, that boasts of 1,000 Chinese students and in 2014 received President Xi Jinping, refused to give Gyatso an honorary degree agreed upon previously. In 2013, the prestigious University of Sydney withdrew its sponsorship from an event where the Dalai Lama was to be the school's guest of honor.

It could be argued that the language institutes and Chinese students at these universities exerted such a deep cultural influence that they convinced the rectors that the Dalai Lama, the "separatist" forced into exile in India since 1959, is socially dangerous. The truth is that ideas and culture have little or nothing to do with these episodes. The power exerted by the Chinese government through the mobilization of its students abroad is neither hard nor soft. It is rather a subtle and obstinate work of propaganda, that together with economic leverage that is anything but negligible (trade relations with North Carolina, abundant funding of the Confucius Institutes, and diplomatic relations in the other cases cited) takes root abroad and produces the desired results. In the last 30 years, the term soft power, regardless of the extraordinary academic works produced by Joseph Nye, has been used by the media and academic worlds as a catch-all term, useful to explain any manifestation of power that does not strictly coincide with the use of military force. Fascinated by the myth of globalization and a world where conflict between states recedes when faced with the benefits of trade, the web and cultural exchanges, analysts and political scientists have seriously underestimated an aspect of power than cannot be reduced to the (per se positive) dimension of ideas. Thus, with the specious intent to expand its soft power, authoritarian countries like China, Russia and Iran have spent billions of dollars to manipulate information and public opinion abroad.

This is nothing new, the reader will note. After all, history is full of examples of states that invest resources to project a positive image abroad. But the phenomenon we submit to your attention has its own historical distinctiveness and deserves to be dealt with separately. These states, where true freedom of opinion is lacking, as is the full benefit of civil and political rights, are not so much interested in improving their reputation. Rather, their goal is to delegitimize the very foundation of democratic states, making their limits and contradictions emerge. The trend is global, and the results are under everyone's eyes. The image of the strong man, the creation of a common enemy, the narrative of "us against them" of illiberal regimes, exert an increasingly strong attraction outside of their national borders. Channeled by the media, universities, conferences and part of their citizens resident abroad, authoritarian rhetoric succeeds in appearing "sexy," and assuming the likeness of soft power, of spontaneous and fruitful cultural exchange. As the director of the Eurasia Group Ian Bremmer wrote in a front-page editorial for *Time*:

> In every region of the world, changing times have boosted public demand for more muscular, assertive leadership. These tough-talking populists promise to protect "us" from "them." Depending on who's talking, "them" can mean the corrupt elite or the grasping poor; foreigners or members of racial, ethnic or religious minorities. Or disloyal politicians, bureaucrats, bankers or judges. Or lying reporters. Out of this divide, a new archetype of leader has emerged.[3]

In November 2017 a group of scholars aimed to bring this form of power into focus, to distinguish it once and for all from soft power and eliminate any alibis for those who exert it. There is a new face of power that cannot be ignored. It is *sharp power*. Like a sharp knife, it "pierces, penetrates, or perforates the information and political environments in the targeted countries."[4]

The link with authoritarian regimes

The long report *Sharp Power. Rising Authoritarian Influence* published by the National Endowment for Democracy (NED), an American non-profit association that deals with the supervision and strengthening of democratic institutions, hit the international debate like a bolt from the blue. The study, published together with the International Forum for Democratic Studies, denounces the attempt of states such as Russia and China to extend their influence abroad with propaganda actions that are silent, but very effective. The secret of their success, we read in the introduction by Christopher Walker and Jessica Ludwig, is the exploitation of "a glaring asymmetry." Internally, these states limit freedom of expression, they censure dissent, and block the market with state monopolies, asking foreign investors to pay the price of significant sharing of technological know-how in order to work in the country. Abroad, though, they can benefit from all of the opportunities that the cultural and financial globalization of the twenty-first century has brought, almost undisturbed: invest money to export domestic media platforms, often under strict governmental control; buy companies and equity stakes without having to fear excessive market obstruction; and conduct campaigns to delegitimize democratic systems, even reaching the paradox of accusing them of being illiberal regimes. Nothing out of the ordinary, the reader may say again.

State propaganda, as we have noted, has always existed. It would be short-sighted and maybe even ridiculous to deny that proven democracies such as the United States, France or Germany have not made use of propaganda in the past 50 years. There is a fundamental distinction, though, that is useful to clarify the difference between democratic states and illiberal states.

In the first case, freedom of expression allows the press, the opposition and civil society to monitor the conduct of state actors, denounce their false steps and mobilize public opinion. For every person who looks the other way when faced with injustice and iniquity due to those in power, there still exists a system of checks and balances sufficient to expose power and keep it in the spotlight. In illiberal regimes this possibility is reduced to a minimum, or is entirely absent. A example from the recent past can help us understand the question. In 2002, under the George W. Bush Administration, the Pentagon launched the "military analyst program." The Defense Department's plan called for the ad hoc training of hundreds of military analysts, former officers and lobbyists, so they would spread a narrative that was favorable to the Pentagon's view of the Iraq War, through television channels and newspapers. These *message force multipliers* – as they were defined in the Defense documents – presented themselves on TV as independent analysts, praising the deeds of the US Army in Iraq and defending the legitimacy of the prison at Guantanamo. In 2008, David Barstow published the documents of the program in the *New York Times*, presenting a long investigation which explained the origins of the plan and denouncing those responsible.[5] Without the investigative journalism of the *New York Times*, that won Barstow his third Pulitzer Prize, today we would not be aware of the Pentagon operation and there would not have been two investigations on the subject, by the Government Accountability Office and the Federal Communications Commission, respectively. Not all countries would permit an investigative journalist to publish government documents and criticize the leaders of the executive and the army. We can only imagine how problematic it would be for a journalist to produce a similar investigation in Russia, China or Turkey.

The myth of soft power as the only dimension of power opposed to military hard power in the age of globalization and free trade (certainly not evoked by Joseph Nye, but by those who interpret him incorrectly or use his work for political purposes), has created fertile ground for authoritarian regimes. Today such countries can promote not only products beyond their borders, but also culture, diplomacy and the propaganda system they use to manage freedom of expression domestically. They do this through instruments that are apparently innocuous: schools, cultural centers, investments and multilateral institutions. But the predominantly political aims of such information exchange contradict their supposed innocence. Reducing them to simple manifestations of cultural influence is a dangerous gamble. What has happened is that many of the most eminent social scientists and political analysts, who as scholars of power and its dimensions should be the first to recognize changes, rested on the laurels of soft power, which is a robust and brilliant theoretical construct, but is no longer sufficient by itself to explain reality. This has led to the creation of what Walker and Ludwig, in the introduction to the NED report, call a "dangerous complacency" towards these undue intrusions in the life of democratic countries.

How can we react? It is possible to raise barriers, limit cultural exchange and break off diplomatic relations with states suspected of interfering abroad to undermine the very legitimacy of democracies. An eye for an eye, a tooth for a tooth. Yet in this way the risk is to lower ourselves to the same level as illiberal regimes, washing away all of the benefits that honest cooperation with these states can provide on an economic and cultural level. A witch-hunt is of no use, except to give new life to those who are already working to destroy the narrative of democratic countries. Thus, the only tool that remains is to increase awareness of the danger, expose interference by these states (which is widespread, but still limited), and raise the level of alert in the academic, business and political worlds.

This need led to the NED study at the end of 2017: four case studies (Argentina, Peru, Poland and Slovakia) managed by four scholars, that in the pages that follow will prove useful to provide a concrete idea of what sharp power is. The NED study is certainly not impartial. The conservative think tank based in Washington was created in 1983 with the support of Ronald Reagan, who was always in favor of "strengthening democratic institutions."[6] The NED has been the subject of criticism over the years from American politicians and intellectuals, but most of the accusations against the think tank come from abroad, principally from the countries that are the target of the published research. In July 2015, the NED was the first NGO expelled from Russia following a decree signed by President Vladimir Putin with the aim of eliminating "undesirable NGOs," without a decision of the courts. In a press release, the office of the Deputy Prosecutor General of Russia Vladimir Malinovsky justified the expulsion with the fact that the NED allegedly "participated in work to declare the results of election campaigns illegitimate, organize political actions intended to influence decisions made by the authorities, and discredit service in Russia's armed forces."[7]

The status of the debate

Apart from any political considerations, the report on sharp power is the result of meticulous work carried out for months by the authors. The enclosed documentation and the details that enrich it were intended to dispel any doubts regarding ideological prejudice in the study. As was to be expected, though, it took only a few weeks for a lively international debate to be triggered around the arguments of the American researchers. At first, the discussion remained within the confines of the United States academic community. When it was picked up in *Foreign Affairs* and then the *Economist*, the study soon drew the attention of Joseph Nye. The Harvard professor responded to the NED's theories with two articles. In his view, the sharp power of authoritarian regimes can in no way be a substitute for their soft power, nor does it take anything away from the power of culture as a diplomatic tool. "Sharp power, the deceptive use of information for hostile purposes, is a type of hard power," wrote Nye in the magazine of the Council of Foreign Relations, "[...] What's new is not the basic model; it's the speed with which such disinformation can spread and the low cost of spreading it."[8] According to Nye, an overreaction to the intrusions of countries such as Russia and China entails two types of risks. The first is to underestimate the immense benefits deriving from frank and free cultural exchange with these countries. The restriction of freedom of expression and the use of state propaganda in their civil societies must not lead us to ignore the extraordinary cultural wealth and economic opportunities that characterize these nations. Secondly, to join them on the same ground, that of sharp power, would be extremely counterproductive: "it would be a mistake for them to imitate the authoritarians and launch major programs of covert information warfare. Such actions would not stay covert for long and when revealed would undercut soft power."[9] The analyst then returned to the theme in an interview with *Formiche*.[10] "Sharp power," he said, "is only a new term to indicate what we once called information warfare, that has existed for decades, and in particular since the 1930s and during the Cold War. Information warfare cannot replace the ability to attract other countries through soft power."

It did not take long for the debate to go beyond the universities and enter the world of politics, provoking conflicting reactions. In December 2017, Republican Senator Marco Rubio, who had been a candidate in the 2016 presidential primaries, called a meeting of the Congressional

Executive Commission on China with a session entitled "The Long Arm of China: Exporting Authoritarianism with Chinese Characteristics." On March 21, 2018, following a continuous debate, the US House and Senate approved two bills aimed at undermining foreign propaganda: the *Countering Foreign Propaganda Act* and the *Foreign Influence Transparency Act*.[11] With the new laws taking effect, foreign organizations such as the Confucius Institutes will be forced to register under the *Foreign Agents Registration Act* before being able to operate in the US[12] The debate had an even more explosive impact in Australia, where distrust towards the Chinese community has grown considerably since the beginning of 2018, after the government in Canberra officially accused Beijing of manipulating Australian politics, causing an outcry in the country of the Dragon.[13] For its part, the Chinese government pointed towards the NED report, accusing the Americans of discriminating against China based on a long-term, unfounded ideological prejudice. On March 3, 2018, Wang Guoqing, spokesman of the Chinese People's Political Consultative Conference (CPPCC), the highest consultative body in China, expressed Beijing's indignation over the narrative of sharp power: "Even though we are talking about exactly the same thing, for Western countries, they are showcasing soft power or smart power. But when it comes to China, it's sharp power or ulterior motives."[14] After the party, the counterattack shifted to the media world, which for the most part is controlled by the CPC. Thus the Chinese state press agency Xinhua branded the American study as "a language trap, coined and manipulated by some Western countries with 'zero-sum' mentality and cultural hegemony." The same line was followed by *Global Times*, the international arm of the party newspaper, the *People's Daily*. Sharp power, we read in a fiery editorial from the end of January 2018, is nothing but "a pseudo-academic concept useful for confirming Western biases."[15]

The echo on the Old Continent

There was a certain echo of the debate on the Old Continent. In January, the head of Security of the European Commission, Julian King, launched an alarm regarding a vast Russian disinformation campaign, claiming that the European Union had identified at least "3,500 cases of pro-Kremlin disinformation contradicting publicly-available facts in multiple languages and on multiple occasions." The announcement of the creation of a task force of experts at the Commission to identify and combat the disinformation spread by Moscow's government media outlets triggered a harsh discussion among Europarliamentarians on the appropriateness of the initiative, with some exaggerations. Some journalistic accounts reached the point of accusing the Russian Federation of having interfered, more or less directly, in the Brexit referendum of June 2016, and even in the Italian elections of March 4, 2018. No concrete proof has been given for those accusations, which as was to be expected, have contributed to strengthening the Russian narrative of the West being prejudicially lined up against Moscow. This is one of the reasons that the Commission completed the work of the task force, publishing a report in March that lists the most frequent threats and a series of solutions to prevent them, without mentioning Russia even once.[16]

Launching *erga omnes* accusations risks jeopardizing the prevention of hybrid threats and Russian government propaganda. The rhetoric becomes bizarre when there is an attempt to trace any election result in a European country to the work of manipulation by the Kremlin. In a recent report, the European Council on Foreign Relations (ECFR) clearly summarized the danger of being exposed to Moscow's anti-Western narrative.

> This tendency of interpreting every election or event through the Russian lens is counterproductive. Russian efforts can only play on pre-existing social cleavages. Arguably, their efforts can amplify existing tensions, but most European societies are proving quite adept at polarizing themselves.
> Reducing everything to Russian meddling leads to dangerous neglect of the real issues behind home-grown polarization and encourages demagogic politicians to use the threat from Russia opportunistically.[17]

At the same time, it is impossible to deny the success that the vast range of methods and strategies of pressure provides the Russian government. A report of the NATO Parliamentary Assembly of March 27, 2018 addresses the Kremlin's "hybrid war" on the Old Continent.[18] It is hybrid in terms of form and content, because the war is "kinetic," cyber, informational and political. We will only examine the last three dimensions here, those that do not entail the intervention of contractors or paramilitary groups without a flag to carry out the missions. As we will see in detail in Chapter 3, Russian sharp power takes the form of a forced change in the narrative aimed at inducing European states, as well as others, to distrust the Western model, to look suspiciously on multilateral institutions and in particular on the United States. The government in Moscow has never hidden its desire to use hybrid and information warfare as part of its national security strategy. Obviously, within the country these operations are presented from the standpoint of the West's anti-Russian narrative, and thus as necessary tools of defense. Numerous public documents in Russia, such as the Military Doctrine of 2014, the National Security Strategy and the Doctrine of Information Security of 2015 demonstrate the importance that information warfare holds in the Kremlin's strategy, and refer more or less explicitly to "non-traditional" methods to influence public opinion abroad. Back in 2013, General Valery Gerasimov, Chief of Staff of the Russian armed forces, listed among the new instruments for war "simultaneous warfare in all physical environments and the information space," in an article that became known under the name of the "Gerasimov Doctrine." Despite recognizing the danger of underestimating Russian hybrid warfare, at the same time the NATO report suggests not overestimating these phenomena. There are two good reasons to follow this advice. First of all, it should be stressed once again that "the Kremlin's interference does not create new societal cleavages or negative trends, it merely tries to reinforce them." Secondly, it is important to avoid falling into collective hysteria that flags the Russian threat as the origin of any social and political conflict that has arisen in Europe in recent years. "Exaggerating the impact of Russian meddling," writes the NATO rapporteur, "could, in fact, be counterproductive as it could make the Kremlin more important than it really is."

If for obvious historical reasons the discussion of Russian strategy for influence has occupied European diplomacy for decades, the same cannot be said of Chinese sharp power. The waves provoked by the NED researchers have truly stirred things up among European policymakers. An initial sign of the danger was recognized in November 2017, when the *Financial Times* wrote that Springer Nature, a German company that is a global leader in scientific publications, had removed more than 1,000 articles from the Chinese market because they were not compatible with Beijing's censorship.[19] All of the articles in question contained key words such as "Tibet," "Taiwan" or "Cultural Revolution." Two months earlier, a similar decision had been made by the prestigious publisher Cambridge University Press, that then reversed its position, though. A second episode, again in Germany, brought China under the spotlight of European public opinion. In December 2017, the Federal Office for Protection of the Constitution (BfV), the intelligence agency of the German Ministry of the Interior, accused Beijing of using social networks to extract information from citizens, parliamentarians and workers in the public administration in Germany. According to the BfV, Chinese agents created false LinkedIn profiles to offer work and expensed trips to China for conferences and meetings with important businessmen in exchange for information on German foreign policy. Obviously, the accusations were promptly denied. Lu Kang, the spokesman for the Chinese Foreign Ministry, immediately responded with strong words: "We expect that agencies which are so important in Germany will speak and behave more responsibly, rather than acting to the detriment of bilateral relations."[20] The long trail of discussions over the Dragon's alleged improper behavior in Europe led the European Parliament itself to take a position, although softly, by publishing a brief document entitled *China's Foreign Influence Operations in Western Liberal Democracies: An Emerging Debate*.[21]

What worries European diplomats is not such much the undue influence in the academic and cultural worlds, which is fairly limited today, but the financial aspect of Chinese expansion in Europe. According to a *Bloomberg* study, in the last ten years China has invested more than 318 billion dollars in the Old Continent.[22] Many of the business groups or corporations that have been the subject of Beijing's financial operations were strategic assets in the respective states.

Worries are growing around the One Belt One Road project (OBOR), the colossal Chinese infrastructure plan to build a new Silk Road and thus unite Europe, the Middle East and Asia to favor investment flows and international trade. This is an extraordinary opportunity for Asian countries to make up the infrastructure gap in the coming years, but above all to exponentially increase free trade between European states and Asia and create an unprecedented network of cultural exchange. Yet a huge project such as OBOR cannot but raise some reservations in the dozens of countries that, whether they like it or not, will be affected by the new land and maritime routes. Chinese Foreign Minister Wang Yi has attempted to provide public reassurances on this point: "There is no back-room deal; everything is transparent. There is no 'winner takes all'; every project delivers win-win results."[23] Yet the leaders of European powers are not convinced that investments coming from the Dragon are apolitical. The first to raise the question was Chancellor Angela Merkel in February 2018, when on a visit to Macedonia she admitted that she had no objections "to the fact that China wants to trade ... and to invest," but added that it would not be in the spirit of free trade if "economic relations were linked with political questions."[24]

One operation that drew criticism from European political figures is the 2017 purchase by COSCO (Chinese Ocean Shipping Company), the Chinese state group that is a global leader in shipping and logistics services, of 51 percent of the historic port of Piraeus in Greece, a *"Dragon*-head" of the Belt and Road Initiative (BRI). Beijing's mission was successful, not only in financial terms. The government of Athens has shown signs of gradual rapprochement with China's government, that can now count on a solid ally within the EU. The peak of this strategic alignment may have been reached in June 2017, when Greece vetoed an EU declaration at the UN against the violation of human rights in China. This was an unprecedented event, that convinced Brussels and the other member states of the need to regain the trust of the Greek government and people before it is too late.

An unprecedented threat

The debate over sharp power, despite all of its possible deficiencies, has the merit of bringing us to a factual observation. We are facing a revolution in the science of international relations. Attempting to interpret the battle for cultural hegemony that characterizes our century in light of multilateral cooperation and the exchanges allowed by globalization does not appear to be very realistic. There is no state in history, whether democratic or an authoritarian regime, that can claim not to be involved in the race for power in the international arena. The IT revolution and globalization have, however, introduced new instruments to reach the goal. Winning over the public opinion of another state is the first step to finding new political military and economic allies. Some of the instruments are conventional: diplomacy, democratic multilateral institutions, trade – provided it is free and reciprocal – and the sharing of culture. Others, if used with hostile intentions, are just as effective: the manipulation of news, information warfare, economic supremacy, pressure on political leaders and cyber attacks. Raising the alert level, avoiding at all costs the risk of falling into alarmism or ideological battles, helps distinguish the different types of instruments.

Sharp power has three dimensions. The first is to win over, at all costs, public opinion and the institutions that channel it: schools, universities, think tanks, media and social networks. The second area where sharp power shows its effects is politics: thus political parties, but also multilateral institutions, single policymakers, foundations and lobbying groups. The third arena is that of economics, which is often the most decisive. Investments and trade agreements are not always made to earn financial profits. Projects with the dimensions of OBOR can become a precious soft power resource for China, and vice versa, for European culture in Asia. Yet more than one country has alleged that the gigantic infrastructure plan is based on a political design. This is true in the case of India, that fears an increase of the Chinese military presence in the region, the forced sharing of know-how with Beijing in the infrastructure construction phase, and above all the Karakorum highway, that would join Western China to the Pakistani plains, passing through a territory historically contested between New Delhi and Islamabad, Gilgit-Baltistan, that was once part of the principalities of Jammu and Kashmir.

The cyber dimension of sharp power brings the other three cited dimensions together, and deserves to be treated separately due to the scope of the phenomenon and the danger it represents. We have attempted to reconstruct the origins and characteristics traits of sharp power. In Chapter 3, a treatment of the phenomenon through concrete examples from recent years will help us understand the dynamics more in depth. The NED study shed light on a situation gravely underestimated by the academic world. It would be reductive, though, to believe that sharp power is a weapon in the hands of only two states, China and Russia. The range of authoritarian states that make use of unconventional strategies to extend their influence abroad is much broader. In addition, there is an aspect of sharp power that states with solid democratic institutions do not eschew: the use of economic and diplomatic power. Acknowledging this allows us to abandon political analysis burdened by politically correct thinking, and study a paradigm shift in international relations that affects all great powers, excluding none.

Notes

[1] D. Goldin, "China says no talking Tibet as Confucius funds US universities," *Bloomberg.com*, 2/11/2011, www.bloomberg.com.

² *Ibid.*
³ I. Bremmer, "The 'strongmen era' is here. Here's what it means for you," *Time*, 3/5/2018, time.com. See also I. Bremmer, *Us vs. Them: The Failure of Globalism*, London, Portfolio, 2018.
⁴ National Endowment for Democracy, International Forum for Democratic Studies, *Sharp Power. Rising-Authoritarian Influence, December 2017*, www.ned.org, p. 13.
⁵ D. Barstow, "Behind TV analysts, Pentagon's hidden hand," *New York Times*, 20/4/2008, www.nytimes.com.
⁶ Reagan pronounced this sentence in a famous speech to the British Parliament on June 8, 1982. For the full text, see "Text of Reagan's address to parliament on promoting democracy," www.nytimes.com.
⁷ A. Luhn, "National Endowment for Democracy is first 'undesirable' NGO banned in Russia," *The Guardian*, 28/7/2015, www.theguardian.com.
⁸ J.S. Nye Jr, "How sharp power threatens soft power," *Foreign Affairs*, 24/1/2018, www.foreignaffairs.com.
⁹ *Ibid.*
¹⁰ F. Bechis, "Così Donald Trump sta minando il soft power americano. Intervista esclusiva a Joseph Nye," *Formiche.net*, 12/1/2018, www.formiche.net.
¹¹ *Countering Foreign Propaganda Act of 2018*, https://stefanik.house.gov/sites/stefanik.house.gov/files/MOULTO_063_xml2.pdf; *Foreign Influence Transparency Act*, https://www.rubio.senate.gov/public/_cache/files/ac28ef8d-ce17-40da-9236-9810706a4ec4/1830D34EB93227A2E 053BE3E4F7E37DD.aeg18195.pdf.
¹² *Foreign Agents Registration Act* (FARA), https://www.justice.gov/nsd-fara.
¹³ B. Birties, "China lodges official complaint after Malcolm Turnbull's comments about foreign interference," *ABC News*, 9/12/2017, http://www.abc.net.au.
¹⁴ D. Cheong, "'Sharp power' allegations part of efforts to smear China: Beijing," *Straits Times*, 3/3/2018, www.straitstimes.com.
¹⁵ L. Si, "Spotlight: 'Sharp power' or Western invisible power," *Xinhua*, 13/2/2018, www.xinhuanet.com.
¹⁶ European Commission, *Final Report of the High Level Expert Group on Fake News and Online Disinformation*, 12/3/2018, ec.europa.eu.
¹⁷ K. Liik, *Winning the Normative War with Russia: An EU–Russia Power Audit*, European Council on Foreign Relations, 21/5/2018, http:// www.ecfr.eu.
¹⁸ M. Joplin, *Countering Russia's Hybrid Threats: An Update*, NATO Parliamentary Assembly, 27/3/2018, www.nato-pa.int.
¹⁹ "Outcry as latest global publisher bows to China," *Financial Times*, 31/10/2017, www.ft.com.
²⁰ "Germany says China seeking to ensnare officials on social networks," *Financial Times*, 10/12/2017, www.ft.com.
²¹ European Parliament, *China's Foreign Influence Operations in Western Liberal Democracies: An Emerging Debate*, http://www.europarl.europa.eu.
²² A. Tartar et al., "How China is buying its way into Europe," *Bloomberg.com*, 23/4/2018, www.bloomberg.com.
²³ Ministry of Foreign Affairs of the People's Republic of China, *Foreign Minister Yi meets the Press*, 9/3/2018, www.fmprc.gov.cn.
²⁴ "Merkel warns against China's influence in Balkans," *South China Morning Post*, 22/2/2018, www.scmp.com.

3   The ABCs of Sharp Power

"If your plan is for one year, plant rice. If your plan is for ten years, plant trees. If your plan is for one hundred years educate children."[1] This is one of the many, perhaps too many, phrases attributed to Confucius, the famous Chinese thinker of the principality of Lu who lived between the sixth and fifth centuries bc. We do not know for certain if the hermit philosopher pronounced these words. We do know, however, that the Chinese government, that during Mao's Cultural Revolution (1966–76) opposed and even banned the cult of Confucius, has literally made this one of its maxims for almost 15 years. In November 2004, Hu Jintao's China inaugurated the first Confucius Institute in Seoul, South Korea. Coordinated and controlled by Hanban, the office of the International Council for Chinese language at the Ministry of Culture, the institutes were presented to the world with great emphasis by the Forbidden City. After years of economic and cultural isolation, Hu's China launched a global initiative to foster knowledge of not only Chinese language abroad, but also of Chinese culture and traditions. The choice of the name Confucius is perfect for this purpose, because in mass culture the Chinese philosophy represents a positive and well-regarded image of the Dragon. If they had been called the Mao institutes, they probably would not have enjoyed the same fortune. Using the tradition, thought and ancient customs of China is part of a strategy that Xi Jinping, much more than those preceded him as head of the party, has decided to implement in recent years.

The model used as reference for the Confucius Institutes was apparently supposed to be that of many other cultural institutes that consolidate the soft power of states in other countries: the British Council, the Goethe Institut, the Alliance Française and the Instituto Cervantes, to cite only the best-known. The success of the Confucius Institutes has undoubtedly been greater. Today there are 580 Chinese language institutes in the world, in a total of 142 host countries. If these are added to the single satellite classes present in universities, the dimensions of the network become impressive. The institutes are a true jewel for Beijing, that through Hanban can count on the direct collaboration of prestigious Western universities such as the London School of Economics, Stanford and Columbia. Some are characterized by concentrating mostly on economics, while others offer courses in medicine, and others still host exhibits, dancing and cooking classes. Officially, the common mission is to promote Chinese culture abroad. This is a task that the centers controlled by Hanban fulfill industriously by attempting to dispel the fear of a "Chinese threat," which is rather widespread in Western media, showing the face of a China that is culturally open, peaceful and undergoing continuous economic growth. In a nutshell, their goal is to facilitate Chinese soft power abroad, as expressly required by the most recent version of the CPC constitution.

Fourteen years after the foundation of the first Confucius Institute, the seed has borne fruit. The most striking case is probably Africa, where more than 40 institutes have been built. Hanban's work on the continent has acted as a driver for Chinese influence together with an enormous volume of investments from Beijing. Thus, while in Western universities criticism first began to spread with regard to the Chinese cultural centers, Beijing saw the consolidation of its soft power on the Black Continent. The results reached on both sides of the Indian Ocean are notable. China represents the top destination for Anglophone African students desiring an experience abroad. And the institutes have made the Dragon truly fashionable in countries seeking a rapid path to development such as Zimbabwe, Zambia or Mozambique, where the number of students who make a foray into Mandarin, to then study in China, is constantly increasing. Moreover, the study grants offered by Hanban represent a considerable incentive for families that cannot guarantee an education abroad for their children.

The success of the Confucius Institutes is not limited to African countries. In South America the number of institutes established amounts to 39, for a total enrollment of 100,000 students. The United States leads the rankings with 110 institutes, followed by the United Kingdom, Australia and Italy.[2] To demonstrate the global nature of the initiative, it is interesting to note that the three headquarters of the Confucius Institutes built by

Hanban are not in Asia, but in America and Europe. The Washington, DC center focuses on lobbying activities, London on the publication of teaching materials, and Santiago del Cile on the promotion of cultural activities in cooperation with other national institutes.

There are various reasons why a university decides to host a Confucius Institute. Granting Hanban a space inside the walls of a university is a winning hand for good diplomatic relations with Beijing. More often, though, the opening of an institute is based on a very pragmatic calculation. The inauguration of a center inside a university is in fact almost entirely funded by Hanban. The host university must provide the offices and facilities, and participate in the training of the board of directors. On the other hand, the selection of the personnel, as well as of the Chinese director, follows rigid criteria listed in the constitution drawn up by Hanban. To this point, it could seem that the university that decides to host an institute has nothing to lose, and everything to gain. The judgment of the Hanban network is reversed, however, if we observe the Confucius Institutes from the standpoint of sharp power, and not as engines of that Chinese cultural "charm offensive" which Joshua Kurlantzick spoke of in the past.[3]

The suspicion that the sophisticated organization of the Chinese Cultural Ministry conceals the propaganda of the Communist Party of China is more than justified. It was a high-level official of the Politburo, Li Changchun, Minister of Propaganda from 2002 to 2012, who defined the classes and the Confucius Institutes as "an important part of China's overseas propaganda set-up."[4] The hierarchical structure that governs the institutes cannot but raise some doubts regarding the political independence and freedom of expression of the teachers. The Hanban Board of Directors is in fact made up by 12 Chinese ministers, including the Minister of Foreign Affairs and the head of the agency for press, publications, radio, film and television. For the most part, the Chinese government carries out a careful selection of the teachers and textbooks, that must meet specific value standards.

In recent years, we have seen a crescendo of complaints regarding Confucius Institutes from dozens of universities. In the United States, some schools have passed from words to action, cancelling the agreement that links them to the institutions controlled by Hanban. If the criticisms continue to circulate in the United States, this is due above all to the absence of true freedom of opinion in some classes, denounced by the enrolled students. Indeed, the reports published on the Confucius phenomenon in universities provide grounds for the suspicions. It is unlikely, if not entirely impossible, to find a book that addresses Chinese history and international politics without making use of propaganda terms. Historical events such as the Sino-Japanese War, territorial disputes such as that regarding Tibet, or discussions on respect for human rights in China, when they find room in textbooks, are perfectly in line with the narrative imposed by the Politburo. Obviously, the phenomenon comes in different forms and degrees of intensity depending on the country in question.

It would be unjust to simply write off the validity of the work by Chinese teachers abroad. The dimensions and duration of the protest wave suggest, however, that there are not simply a few bad apples. Sometimes the financial constraints that link host universities to the Confucius Institutes are transformed into a form of political pressure from Beijing. The constitution of the institutes expressly prohibits the universities to which they are linked from "soiling the reputation of the Confucius Institutes," threatening legal action if that occurs.[5] The suspicion, corroborated by a long case record, is that these institutes can consider their reputation to be soiled even when the Dalai Lama is hosted for a lectio magistralis, when a conference is held on the Tiananmen protests, or an exhibit is presented on the Falun Gong religious movement.[6] As incomprehensible as it may seem to us, in China freedom of opinion for the media and the academic world is not contemplated. It is no coincidence that the government uses the word "propaganda" openly, without concealing its aims. To tell the truth, in China "propaganda" is a neutral term, that does not necessarily have a negative connotation. There are various institutions that, more or less explicitly, are dedicated to spreading party propaganda domestically and abroad. Among these, one immediately seems Orwellian: the State Council of Information Office (SCIO). Located in a Soviet-era building in downtown Beijing, the SCIO was born in 1991 with the aim, as the official website states, to "expand the range of Chinese media to introduce China to the international community."[7] Among the body's duties, pursued with a number of personnel and a budget a large multinational would envy, is that of "clarifying and refuting" any article or essay coming from abroad that portrays Chinese businessmen or politicians in a negative light, or deals with thorny issues such as the territorial claims of Hong Kong, Macau and Taiwan.[8] The mere mention of the SCIO produces a dark look on the face of Chinese intellectuals, journalists and professors. However, few seem to be truly surprised by the institution's operations, because by now government censure in China is part of daily life, and everyone needs to deal with it. So this is not the point we wish to address. The key question is to understand to what extent globalization has created that "glaring asymmetry" which Ludwig and Walker speak of in the introduction to the NED report, that allows some illiberal states to export abroad, in a more or less veiled manner, not only culture, tradition and everything that can be desired in an open and frank exchange, but also restrictions on freedom of the press, the propaganda of the single party, and a business culture subjugated to the directives of the Politburo. As David Shambaugh wisely wrote in 2015, Beijing's propaganda should not surprise us, because "in China propaganda is not a derogatory term."[9] With the opening of the country to globalization, the strategy of influence has also changed. The professor continues: "As the country has opened up to the world, the state has had to try harder to maintain its grip on information, and its efforts on this front have become more sophisticated. Now, however, Chinese authorities are trying to control information not only inside China but increasingly outside, too."[10]

It is not possible to change the top-down nature of the Confucius Institutes, or to intervene regarding their strict dependency on the political leaders of Beijing, because that would represent undue interference in the politics of a sovereign country where party propaganda and culture are daily occurrences. That said, monitoring the funding and management methods of these cultural institutes is not only advisable, it is necessary in order to launch a partnership. The quality of textbooks and professors, freedom of opinion in classes, and above all the absence of any political pressure on the surrounding environment must be non-negotiable conditions to begin a lasting relationship between a university and a Hanban institute. Only when these conditions are set can the Chinese charm offensive prove to be an enormous opportunity for growth for countries interested in China's appeal.

Propaganda and sharp power

The *longa manus* of the government over the Hanban circuit has allowed China to strengthen its grip in countries where it was previously entirely absent or viewed with suspicion. In Africa, the work of Chinese institutes and think tanks continues to smooth the way for the mass of Beijing's investments in infrastructure, laying roots in both the academic world and the institutions. Given the dimensions and the continuous expansion of the phenomenon, it is still early to take stock of the operation launched years ago by Hu Jintao. There is no doubt, however, that regardless of the wave of criticism that has hit the Hanban network in the United States and Australia, the experiment can be considered a success for the Dragon. More than 15 years after the opening of the first center in Seoul, the experiment of the Confucius Institutes remains a case to be studied to understand the Chinese government's push for global influence.

It also represents the perfect realization of the old Mao Zedong saying that Xi Jinping decided to revive: "Make the past serve the present, make the foreign things serve China."[11]

However, we should not overestimate the scope of these cultural operations. Despite appearing to be based on propaganda in the eyes of a democratic country, they only represent the handle of a knife called sharp power. There are more direct, incisive and evident instruments which illiberal states such as Russia, China or Iran use to install a precise narrative abroad. Betting on the academic world is an excellent strategy if the goal is to shape public opinion in another country over the long term. Yet the manipulation of media remains the most powerful weapon to immediately win the battle of ideas, possibly playing on pre-existing divisions, uncertainties and sentiments. It is also, and above all, due to the new generation of media that authoritarianism has become global and sexy, a valid alternative to take into consideration especially if compared with a West painted as militarily and economically decadent, internally divided and uncertain regarding its future. It is in the media field that the battle of "us against them" is fought, it is here that an apparently incurable split has been created between the liberal and conservative worlds, between those who want more globalization and those who wave the white flag and promise to avenge the injustices globalization has inflicted on them, between the old "comprador bourgeoisie" and the new national bourgeoisie, to cite Giulio Sapelli.[12] In a world that definitively abandons the analog era to become increasingly digital, online information remains the most effective instrument to win over public opinion. It goes without saying that a state does not invest resources in the world of information with only the goal of manipulating public opinion. There are various examples of large broadcasters entirely managed and funded by government authorities that do an excellent job. We see this in the case of giants such as BBC, Voice of America, Agence France-Presse or Al Jazeera, that receive public financing but still do not suffer surgical censure of their content and tight control by the government over their method of journalistic work. These networks are also not immune to forms of influence from economic and political stakeholders, a dynamic which, it must be said, cannot be avoided by any television or newspaper that is not literally self-sufficient from a financial standpoint. It is one thing, though, to have to follow an editorial line and respect certain criteria in the selection and framing of news; it is another to become the instrument for the implementation of a precise political agenda, sacrificing professionalism and ethics for that purpose. In the countries we are considering here, propaganda is a matter of fact, that should not be a surprise. Yet the emergence of these countries from international isolation after the Cold War and through globalization has allowed party propaganda to become an export product disguised as an anti-conventional narrative and presumed truth to be presented in contrast to traditional media.

"Telling a good story": the Chinese strategy

The Chinese were among the first to recognize the potential of a media campaign on a global scale. When Jiang Zemin was the secretary of the CPC (1989–2002), the state media had already launched a rebranding operation with the goal of gaining additional audience abroad. In 2000, the largest television network in continental China, CCTV, opened a satellite channel dedicated to English mother tongue foreigners (CCTV9). Yet it was with Hu Jintao at the head of the party secretariat (2002–12) that the Dragon showed its claws, launching a true global crusade to ensure space in the media world of other countries.[13] In 2004, CCTV followed in the wake of American information giants such as CNN, or BBC, creating CCTV International from scratch. The result met expectations in terms of budget and geographical penetration, but did less well from the standpoint of censure of contents and political control of journalistic work the year 2009 was the key point to comprehend Beijing's media strategy: the government launched an imposing campaign under the name of "great propaganda" (*da waixuan*), to strengthen the propaganda organs, and in particular Chinese broadcasters operating abroad, with funding of approximately 7.2 billion dollars.[14] The impulse from the party allowed for considerably strengthening the agency Xinhua News Service, that today sits atop the rankings of the largest agencies in the world in terms of number of employees (and is known for lending its employees to intelligence operations), and to launch the English edition of the *Global Times*, the very popular tabloid owned by the *People's Daily*, the party's official newspaper. When Xi Jinping won the secretaryship of the party in November 2012, Chinese propaganda entered a new era. The former governor of Fujian immediately explained that he intended to impose a shift in the way China is spoken of abroad. From his very first speeches as secretary, Xi recalled the importance of telling the world of the "Chinese dream," that of a China that is economically prosperous and militarily strong. He stressed this need without mincing words during the working conference on national propaganda and ideology held in Beijing in August 2013, when he explained that "China should spread new ideas and new perspectives for emerging and developing states," while the media have the task of "telling a good Chinese story" (*jiang yige hao Zhongguo gushi*) and "promoting China's views internationally."[15]

Faced with the recognition of a global crisis of print media, the Chinese media system thus had to take the path indicated by the secretary, betting on the creation of new online information giants, more suited than traditional newspapers to implement the project of creative, digital and global propaganda, in both form and content. Chinese propaganda has thus followed the two indications given by Xi: the centralization of power over the party and the administration in the hands of the secretary, which culminated with the abolishment of the limit of two presidential mandates in March 2018 by the National People's Congress, was followed by a centralization of censure; the attempt to present a China to the world that is renewed, rich, open and ready to act as the standard bearer of globalization was followed by a profound restyling of propaganda. The last step in the Chinese media system's dash to globalization was the maxi-merger between the country's largest TV and radio broadcasters (CCTV, China Radio International and China National Radio) to create a single network that, according to some estimates, has 14,000 employees: Voice of China, a name that clearly refers to the US broadcaster created after the Second World War.[16]

Despite the promise Xi made following his appointment as secretary to expose the corruption of senior officials through the use of the web, he has considerably strengthened the censure of social networks and media abroad. At home, the final guillotine blow to freedom of opinion came with the strengthening of the Great Firewall, the government program introduced in 2006 for the suppression of VPNs (virtual private networks), the private networks that protect inbound and outbound traffic hiding the identity of users and by-passing potential blocks imposed by Chinese government censure. It is no coincidence that the Reporters Without Borders (RWB) press freedom index places the Dragon 176th out of 180 countries, and the same conclusions are reached by various other reports by NGOs such as Freedom House.[17] However creative, global and hi-tech China's propaganda is under Xi, the hold of political censure on the press and civil society has not been relaxed at all.

Information or cyberwarfare? The Russian strategy

Post-Soviet Russia's media strategy is wellknown (and very relevant today) for showing how subtle the boundary can be between political propaganda and information. Russian President Vladimir Putin has never concealed the fact that he intends to be on the front lines of information warfare. In an interview with Russia Today (RT) in 2013, he complemented the new headquarters of the Russian broadcaster, expressing his hope that it would succeed in "try to break the Anglo-Saxon monopoly on the global information streams."[18]

Unlike the global-scale media operation set up by China in the past ten years, the range of influence of Russian information campaigns tends to concentrate on carefully selected regions. Most of the information warfare (*Informatsionnaya Voyna* in Russian, but in Moscow they prefer to call it "information confrontation") is fought in the so-called *Near Abroad*. This expression generically indicates the former Soviet states such as Belarus, Moldova, Ukraine, the Baltic States (Estonia, Latvia, Lithuania) and the states of the Transcaucuses (Georgia, Azerbaijan, Armenia), but in Russian military doctrine it also includes states in Central Asia such as Kazakhstan, Turkmenistan, Uzbekistan and Kyrgyzstan. Obviously, the target of the large Russian pro-government channels does not stop in the surrounding regions. The government media giant *Sputnik* has regional offices in Washington, Cairo, London, Edinburgh and Beijing. Another Russian media giant, RT, broadcasts 24 hours a day in more than ten languages. Yet the most evident political effects of Russian media sharp power are almost all to be seen in the Near Abroad, and in particular in those countries where there is fertile ground for a radical change in the narrative and a break with the past. This explains why Russian propaganda hits with such force in regions that were once the periphery of the Soviet Union. The presence of Russian-speaking communities and generations of descendants of Soviet citizens, together with widespread discontent towards the Western model, facilitates the acceptance of the propaganda message, whose effects can spread under the claim of defending their "fellow countrymen" from the undue influence of the West.

The Kremlin has a broad range of solutions to exercise media sharp power. For the moment we will consider the conventional tools, to then discuss cyber interference in Chapter 4. A recent report on Russian information war identifies three categories of instruments used by Moscow to spread propaganda abroad. The first segment includes "white" means of information, i.e. that for which attribution is easy: the already cited government media Russia Today and *Sputnik*, the state TV All Russia State Television and Radio Broadcasting Company (VGTRK), but also agencies directly controlled by the Ministry of Foreign Affairs are just a few examples.[19] These are the true giants of Russian information, abundantly funded by the Kremlin and present in dozens of countries in the world. The budget and personnel of these agencies are in no way inferior to the foreign competition. Fact-checking and freedom of the press, on the other hand, do not exist. This does not mean that all journalists there are completely controlled by Moscow's propaganda or that there are no true professionals within these organizations; rather, in order to work there one needs to be able to interpret a precise political agenda. The *Sputnik* homepage bears the motto "Telling the untold." Intriguing, isn't it? Too bad that "the untold" is often conspiracy theories, baseless accusations or even fake news created for a specific purpose. Russian media often circulate stories constructed to affect public opinion in European countries where social and political resentment is present. A celebrated case is that of Lisa, the thirteen-year-old German of Russian origin who disappeared in Berlin for a day while returning from school on January 11, 2016. A few hours after her absence was reported by the girl's parents, the correspondent of the very popular Russian state TV channel First Russian TV reported that the girl had been brutally raped by a group of migrants while she was outside of her home. Soon other broadcasters such as *Sputnik* and RT picked up the news, which was widely reported in Russia. Once the incursion into social media had taken place (the Russian correspondent's video went viral), the news triggered an extreme right-wing mobilization to organize street protests against German authorities, accused of having covered up the story due to a politically correct attitude. The echo of the presumed rape was so strong that Russian Foreign Minister Sergey Lavrov decided to address the issue himself during a press conference: "It's clear that the girl did not disappear voluntarily for 30 hours. I hope that these problems are not swept under the carpet and that there'll be no repeat cases like that of our Lisa."[20] Subsequently, the investigators concluded that the girl, as she herself admitted, had not been the subject of any form of violence but had simply decided to spend the night at a friend's house without telling her parents. Lavrov's interference marked a hardening of relations between Moscow and Berlin.

The second segment identified by the report includes "gray" means of information. These are a multitude of websites full of conspiracy theories from both political extremes, sites that contain data or act as containers of articles. It is not easy to trace these aggregators of presumed news to a political authority, but there is no doubt they can play a decisive role in shaping public opinion. Lastly, the third segment embraces the vast universe of "black" information instruments, defined as such because it is extremely difficult to certify and trace them to a precise source. Social networks like Twitter, Telegram and the very popular Russian VKontakte are the preferred grounds for fake news, since it is difficult, if not impossible, to apply journalistic fact-checking to all news that circulates. The mechanism is fairly simple: a fake or at least altered news story channeled through traditional Russian media is picked up by fake contacts created for that purpose (trolls) or by automated contacts (bots) that thus act as force-multipliers in a long "game of telephone" that ends up distorting and expanding their reach thanks to provocative headlines and images that do not correspond to the content. Once they go mainstream in social networks, the news is able to enter the universe of "gray" media we spoke of, and with a bit of luck can catalyze public opinion or even make the homepage of uncareful newspapers.[21] Behind the chain of disinformation there can be lone wolves or actual organizations with a structure and an office.

The most evident example of how fake news can give rise to a true industry is that of the Internet Research Agency (IRA), the Russian troll factory famous for being behind some of the most sensational online disinformation campaigns, that has found itself involved in the Russiagate investigation. According to the documents presented by Robert Mueller one of the funders of the agency is Yevgeny Prigozhin, a powerful oligarch from Saint Petersburg who is very close to Putin and has already been accused of having supported the Russian mercenaries in Crimea (the famous "little green men").[22] The IRA came into the news in 2015 thanks to a long investigation by the *New York Times*, but it had already become famous in Russia for having supported the pro-separatist propaganda at the beginning of the invasion of Crimea.[23] The investigation brought to light both the work of the agency's employees, initially located in a gray Soviet building in a suburb of Saint Petersburg. *The Times* journalist, stationed outside of the entrance, could not believe his eyes. Dozens of employees (but experts speak of thousands around the world) went in and out of the old building with a single task: create fake news and spread it on the web through fake social network profiles or other websites.[24] The number of cases is by now too long to cite here. Suffice it to recall the now famous false alarm of a fire at a chemical plant in St. Mary Parish (Louisiana) in November 2014, spread among residents through trolls and bots. Responsibility for the attack was initially claimed by an alleged ISIS video and relaunched on Twitter by thousands of fake profiles under the hashtag #Columbianchemicals. On the occasion a video was circulated that had been created ad hoc in a recording studio, of a CNN journalist announcing the news of the explosion, and a Wikipedia page was even created, and continuously updated. The FBI was unable to identify the senders of the messages. Yet the coordination, preparation and attention to detail in the operation could not but have come from an organization with considerable human, financial and technological resources.

The impact of Russian online propaganda can sometimes seem irrelevant. Although it is true that even if we were to find fake accounts on social networks or identify disinformation campaigns on the web, it is necessary to avoid tracing the outcome of any election or other appointment in the life of a democratic country to these types of operations, at the same time it is essential not to underestimate the consequences. The means to spread propaganda have changed, but the ultimate goal remains the same. During the Second World War it was done by launching leaflets from airplanes flying above enemy cities. Today thousands of tweets (numbers that a bot can reach in half a day) can be sufficient to upset and misinform part of public opinion, thanks to the right channels, even more so in a moment in which the publishing world is experiencing a profound crisis and web tourists are bombarded 24 hours a day by baseless news or information that is not appropriately verified. At times the fake news that circulates on non-institutional Russian information channels can even make us laugh, at least until we see the ultimate goal. One operation that seemed almost absurd was carried out by Alexander Malkevich, a member of the Civic Chamber of Russia, an advisory body linked to the government. He recently launched USA Really. Wake up Americans, a US web portal sponsored by the Russian state agency Ria Fan, with the solemn objective of combatting "the growing political censure imposed by the United States promoting information and problems that are covered up by the main American publications controlled by the US political elite." As Emanuele Rossi clearly explained on *Formiche.net*, the social network accounts of the new and ambitious pro-Russian portal were blacked out by the operators of the social networks themselves. The apparent misfortune encountered in the social network launch should not deceive us, though: some experts have noted that many of the domains linked to the new information projects were registered through the registrar reg.ru, in the past associated with the cited IRA.[25] Thousands of such portals are being created. The intention, regardless of the actual result, is to create a fake debate, often staging a clash between two opposing factions to reach a predetermined conclusion. Providers and social networks have shown their ability to clear the web of such "bait," making up for the negligent inactivity that allowed them to expand. To do so they need a team of experts. Facebook, for example, announced in August 2018 that it had blocked 652 pages guilty of publishing fake news. With the assistance of the American cybersecurity company FireEye and the DFRLab, the group of debunkers and cyber security experts of the Atlantic Council think tank, the social network created by Mark Zuckerberg, has unearthed a network of supposed information pages originating in Russia, Iran and Latin America.[26] An announcement by Microsoft in that same month is noteworthy. The company attributed the creation of fake websites to the Russian group of hackers APT 28 (we will meet them close up in Chapter 4), known to the public for having hacked the e-mails of Hillary Clinton's election campaign in spring 2016.[27] Well, in this case the target was not the Democrats, but the sites of two respected conservative think tanks, recreated ad hoc by the hackers: the Hudson Institute and the International Republican Institute (the latter's Board of Directors includes such big shots us the

Republican Mitt Romney), not exactly fans of the Trump Administration. Similarly, fake portals have been created of the US Senate. The goal follows the same script: steal the passwords and personal data of the duped users. The powerful Kremlin spokesman Dmitry Peskov, *ça van sans dire*, preferred to evade the accusations from the US web giant: "What hackers are they talking about? We don't know what evidence and basis they have to reach these conclusions."[28] The fact is that the president of Microsoft, Brad Smith, decided to sound the alarm in view of the mid-term elections: "We're concerned that these and other attempts pose security threats to a broadening array of groups connected with both American political parties in the run-up to the 2018 elections."[29]

It was not easy for US intelligence to verify this fear; or at least not as easy as it would have been in the past. As reported by Julian Barnes and Matthew Rosenberg of the *New York Times*, who spoke with high-level officials anonymously, in recent months the American intelligence agencies had to deal with an extremely pragmatic obstacle: fewer and fewer informers from the Kremlin's inner circle are willing to talk.[30] There are many reasons – writes the New York newspaper – behind this slow loss of contacts in Moscow. A role was certainly played by the expulsion by the Russian government of dozens of American diplomats after the break over the Skripal case, the Russian spy poisoned together with his daughter by nerve gas in London on March 4, 2018. It also didn't help, the *New York Times* continues, that there was a certain level of imprudence by the White House; such as when its Intelligence Committee sued the Department of Justice requesting the documentation relating to Stefan A. Halper, a veteran who had probed some Trump campaign officials on behalf of the FBI. The Halper case contributed to dissuade Russian informers from continuing their collaboration with American spies, to not risk ending up in the sights of a harsh counterintelligence campaign carried out by the Kremlin, say the Nyt journalists, including through the use of violent repression.

To understand the importance of not letting our guard down, especially for those who hold important political and institutional positions, it can be useful to tell the story of what recently happened to the former president of the NATO Parliamentary Assembly, Paolo Alli.[31] A call from two famous Russian impersonators, Vladimir Kuznetsov and Alexei Stolyarov (known in Russia as "Vovan" and "Lexus"), risked damaging the reputation and the very security of the Atlantic organization. Perfectly imitating the voice of the president of the Ukrainian Parliament Andriy Parubiy, the two "comedians" called Alli to discuss some NATO matters and lead him to make problematic statements on Russia, thanks to little comments such as "let's hope Putin loses the next elections." After having recorded the voice of the Italian politician, the two repeated the same operation with the Ukrainian official. Fortunately neither Alli nor Parubyi revealed sensitive information during the calls, which to their great surprise appeared a few hours later perfectly transcribed on the *Sputnik* website, where it was presented as a simple telephone joke. The two imitators have targeted other figures from the world of politics or entertainment with their calls, but never a representative of the Russian government, and certainly not President Putin. "We wouldn't prank Putin" they said in an interview with the *Guardian*, "We don't want to harm our country. We don't want unrest here; we don't want to do anything that would help the enemies of Russia."[32]

Not only China and Russia: the Middle East

Russia and China are not the only illiberal states that have recently invested considerable resources for propaganda campaigns beyond their national borders. In the first chapter we already dealt with the case of two media giants from the Middle East, Al Jazeera and Al Arabiya; the first funded by Qatar but at the same time now considered one of the most important networks in the world, partly thanks to a certain level of independence granted to its professionals; the second founded by the United Arab Emirates in 2003 that soon became a regional media power, despite remaining a step behind with respect to its Qatari competition both in terms of geographic reach and journalistic quality. There is, however, another Middle East power that in recent years has invested considerable resources to win over the hearts and minds of public opinion abroad. This is Iran, where the monopolist Islamic Republic of Iran Broadcasting (IRIB) occupies practically all media space, partly because the constitution of the Islamic Republic of Iran expressly prohibits the existence of private television companies. The IRIB network now has offices in more than 20 countries, including France, Belgium, the United States and the United Kingdom, thousands of employees and various channels abroad.[33]

Formally, Iranian state television is independent of the government, but the appointment of the director, made by the Supreme Leader Ali Khamenei, leaves little doubt on the actual degree of freedom of the journalists. Like the Russian and Chinese media giants, IRIB also has the goal of promoting a positive narrative of the Islamic Republic in the world, and at the same time attempting to counter what Khamenei loves to define as the "imperialism of Western media." The group is supported in its task by the Islamic Revolutionary Guard Corps (IRGC, better known by the name of Pasdaran), who in the past put one of their own at the head of the network.[34]

Unlike the Iranian state agency IRNA, that for years has competed with the largest agencies in the world, the state television network has only recently expanded its scope of action, opening the channels Hispan TV and Press TV, in Spanish and English, respectively.[35] The internationalization of the television group under the control of Khamenei has not succeeded in screening it from harsh criticism from abroad. The United States, first with Barack Obama in the White House and then with Donald Trump, has repeatedly threatened to impose sanctions targeting the state television company, accused of sponsoring the violation of human rights through practices such as public confessions of prisoners on live TV. As of this writing, the sanctions have not yet been implemented. A human rights organization based in New York condemned the IRIB because it continues to interfere with satellites to prevent other television channels and international networks from broadcasting in the country.[36] The close dependency on the religious leadership and the propagandistic framing of the news provided on the IRIB's channels have not only stirred protests outside of the country or among NGOs. In January 2018, after the wave of riots resulting from the increase in the cost of living, President Hassan Rouhani himself expressed his doubts on the media coverage by state TV: "The IRIB must echo the nation's opinions, not a single faction."[37]

Sharp cash: the Chinese New Silk Road

To complete our analysis of sharp power and the forms it has taken in recent years in the world and in international relations, we cannot ignore one of the most powerful levers a state has to consolidate its influence abroad: the economy. The Chinese cultural offensive abroad through the network of Confucius Institutes would have an irrelevant impact on the political system of the countries that opened their doors to Hanban if it were not supported by conspicuous investments in the host universities. Nor would the pro-Russian message channeled through the state broadcasters, social networks and think tanks in the Balkans have much success if Moscow did not have economic leverage (starting with energy dependency) over the institutional systems of those countries.

It is useful to distinguish between natural effects and side effects of globalization. The opening of markets to foreign investment, the technological revolution, the transnational exchange of know-how and financial globalization have succeeded in breaking down the walls of economies that were once closed to the market. But the system of international institutions identified to govern the economic transition of these states has not always been successful. The decision-making capacity of the World Trade Organization (WTO), the body in charge of supervising the trade exchanges of 164 countries, has too often been slowed by the mutual vetoes of member states, meaning that on more than one occasion the reciprocity and fair play that characterize the free market have had to succumb to contingent political dynamics. Thus one of the largest side effects of globalization has been to create that "glaring asymmetry" we have already mentioned, that allows states such as China and Russia to use all of the advantages of the free market without losing certain old habits, starting with state dirigisme of the economy and the opening of the internal market to foreign investors only intermittently. This asymmetry grants such states leverage that is more political than economic abroad, without exposing them to the risk of harsh reprisals.

Let us take the case of China, that in recent years has become a target of the United States and President Donald Trump, accused of trade dumping, limiting competition in the Chinese market to a minimum and financing its own enterprises, violating the intellectual property rights of foreign companies and imposing a set of strict conditions on foreign companies that wish to make investments in China. State subsidies, exemptions and inside information provided by the Chinese government to its own businesses rig internal competition and keep alive even companies that due to excess capacity are on the verge of bankruptcy. On the other hand, in recent years China has increased its foreign trade tenfold. According to a recent report, the quantity of Chinese foreign direct investment (FDI) in Europe in 2017 reached a peak of 81 billion dollars, an exorbitant amount if compared with previous years.[38] The same is true for the African continent, where Chinese direct investment has grown exponentially in the last ten years, making the Dragon by far the largest trading partner for Africa. Beijing's growing assertiveness abroad undoubtedly has positive effects, starting with effects on employment that follows investments (in some African states the portion of local workers employed in Chinese companies is as high as 89 percent).[39] At the same time, though, this gives the Chinese government political leverage that is anything but unimportant.

Beijing does not hide the fact that it considers economic policy as a driver of diplomacy. The enormous investment program of the cited One Belt One Road (OBOR) project, the gigantic network of land and sea infrastructure through which the Chinese government wants to unite China, Eurasia, Southeast Asia and Western Africa, is the crystal-clear demonstration of how politics, economics and diplomacy form an inseparable whole for the Dragon. This is a project that gives concrete form, and in practice aims to noticeably go beyond, the "going out" strategy to put its hands on new natural resources and create a global infrastructure network launched in the Jiang era and continued with Hu Jintao and Xi Jinping.[40] The advantages deriving from the construction of a new Silk Road are not limited to trade, however. There are important strategic implications that cannot be ignored. The construction of the 62-billion dollar China–Pakistan Economic Corridor (CPEC), to give an example, that is to unite the region of Xinjiang with the Pakistani port of Gwadar on the Makran coast, is at the center of a heated clash between the Indian and Chinese governments. The only route that would allow the Chinese to reach the Pakistani port is the cited highway of Karakorum, a high-altitude passageway that goes through the territory of Gilgit-Baltistan, once part of the principalities of Jammu and Kashmir, that have always been disputed by India and Pakistan.[41] For New Delhi the CPEC represents a grave violation of its territorial sovereignty. To this we must add the fears, shared by other states, that the corridor will throw open the doors to a stronger Chinese military presence in the region, starting with the construction of a naval base in a strategic port such as Gwadar.

The protests of India are not an isolated case. In February 2018 Admiral Harry Harris, then the head of the United States Pacific Command (USPACOM), warned the Congress of expansion by the Chinese navy through the acquisition of strategic ports along the new Silk Road.[42] Under the umbrella of OBOR investments, Chinese state companies have already gotten their hands on strategically important ports in Greece, Cambodia, Indonesia, Myanmar, Pakistan, Sri Lanka and Djibouti, where next to the port of Doraleh an imposing military base has been built. According to a recent study, the economic profitability of the maxi-acquisitions is very doubtful, while in the Indian Ocean the Silk Road underpins a clear design to expand the range of influence of the Chinese navy.[43] It is thus clear that Chinese economic growth entails winners and losers, opportunities but also dangers, regardless of the reassurances that come from the Forbidden City, that in its official releases and public statements never fails to assure the world of Beijing's desire to seek a path towards growth that is win-win for everyone.

Hitting the gas: the power of energy

Let us leave Asia for a moment and return to the Old Continent, where a game of Risk has been ongoing for decades regarding energy supremacy. The availability of energy resources is one of the most effective tools of sharp power a state can have, to the point that in the academic world by now there is often talk of "energy geopolitics." In the hands of an authoritarian state, an oil or gas deposit can become a lethal weapon to make allies or distract attention from internal politics. This is the conclusion reached by a recent study of the European Parliament:

> Energy resources wielded by authoritarian states can act as a shield or a sword. A dependency relationship exists between an energy supplier and its consumers. When the energy supplier is a (quasi)monopolist in a market, this dependency translates into political leverage. This political leverage can be used either to prevent outside interference and ensure regime survival, or as a tool for an assertive foreign policy. By doing so, the authoritarian state can use energy supplies as a means to condition neighboring countries to behave in a certain way, or to punish them when they do not.[44]

There are various examples that can be drawn from recent history. The most sensational remains the 1973 oil embargo in which right after the Yom Kippur War the OPEC countries (Iran, Iraq, United Arab Emirates, Saudi Arabia, Qatar and Kuwait) raised oil prices and cut exports towards countries that were friends of Israel, causing a fourfold increase in the global price of oil. Yet there are many more examples. A recent one is the Baku–Tbilisi–Ceyhan (BTC) gas pipeline that links the Caspian Sea to the Mediterranean through Azerbaijan, Georgia and Turkey, constructed at the start of the 2000s with the precise aim of bypassing the territory of Armenia, an enemy of Turkey and Azerbaijan since the beginning of the Nagorno-Karabakh conflict.

However, nobody in Europe has the dominant energy power of Russia, that for decades has been the top supplier of gas to the Old Continent. Fifteen member states of the European Union depend on Moscow for more than half of their gas needs. This dominant position has allowed the Russian government to open and close the faucets over the years, or even only threaten to do so, to pressure the European Union and pursue its own foreign policy agenda. Little or nothing has been achieved by the EU sanctions against Russia due to violation of the Minsk agreements, partly because the package of restrictive measures does not affect the conventional energy sector. There is a vast range of instruments with which the Russian government can exercise political pressure on European states and the Near Abroad, through giants in the sector such as Gazprom and Rosneft, from the control of the infrastructure that brings the gas to Europe, to the manipulation of prices, to the insertion into contracts of clauses that categorically prohibit the sale of the gas to third countries (for example posing an ultimatum to European countries: receive Russian gas without being able to resell it to Ukraine, or side with Kiev and accept the consequences). For their part, the Russian energy giants have always sought a certain alignment with the foreign policy agenda of the motherland, showing more flexibility with states close to Moscow and much less towards enemies of the Russian government. In December 2013, Vladimir Putin offered Ukrainian President Viktor Yanukovych a discount on Gazprom supplies after the Ukrainian government decided to enter the pro-Russian Eurasian Economic Union (EEU), while the protestors were already filling the streets of Kiev. As soon as the new Ukrainian President Petro Poroshenko backtracked, Gazprom raised prices again and cut supplies. More recently, much discussion has been provoked by the Nord Stream 2 project, the gas pipeline that will connect Moscow to Germany passing through the Baltic Sea. The Ukrainian government has denounced the plan, that seems conceived specifically to cut Ukraine out from the route. On this question, though, it has not found decisive support from European allies, who will actively participate in the construction of the pipeline.[45] It will certainly be difficult to find support in Germany, that has invested heavily in Nord Stream 2 and depends on Russian supplies for over 50 percent of its gas needs. With the Baltic Sea pipeline this special relationship risks becoming irreversible and weighing heavily on European foreign policy. This does not please the Europe's ally, the United States, at all. At the July 2018 NATO summit President Trump warned Angela Merkel of the risk of becoming a "hostage" to the Kremlin: "Berlin pays billions of dollars to Russia for energy supplies and we have to pay to defend them against Russia?" As usual, his brusque tone caused a stir; but there is no doubt that the question is well posed.

Notes

[1] D. Torres, "China's soft power offensive," *Politico*, 26/12/2017, www. politico.eu.

[2] Hanban, *About Confucius Institute/Classroom*, english.hanban.org.

[3] J. Kurlantzick, *Charm Offensive: How China's Soft Power is Transforming the World*, New Haven, Yale University Press, 2007.

[4] B. Allen-Ebrahimian, "House proposal targets Confucius Institutes as foreign agents," *Foreign Policy*, 14/3/2018, foreignpolicy.com.

[5] Hanban, *Constitution and by-laws of the Confucius Institutes*, Cap. 7, art. 36 c, english.hanban.org.

[6] In 2008 an Israeli district court convicted the University of Tel Aviv, where a Confucius Institute is present, for having illegally cancelled an exhibit on Falun Gong, a spiritual movement born in China at the beginning of the 1990s and repressed by the Chinese government. During the trial the rector Yoav Ariel admitted that he had received pressure from the Chinese Embassy to close the exhibit: O. Edelman, "Court: TAU bowed to Chinese pressure over Falun exhibition," *Haaretz*, 1/10/2009, www.haaretz.com.

[7] The State Council Information Office, The People's Republic of China, *About SCIO*, english.scio.gov.cn.

[8] *Testimony of Associate-Professor Anne-Marie Brady School of Political and Social Sciences University of Canterbury, Christchurch, New Zealand US-China Economic & Security Review Commission China's Propaganda and Perception Management Efforts, Its Intelligence Activities that Target the United States, and the Resulting Impacts on US National Security 30 April*, 2009, p. 3, www.uscc.gov

[9] D. Shambaugh, "China's soft-power push," *Foreign Affairs*, July–August 2015, www.foreignaffairs.com.

[10] *Ibid.*

[11] A.-M. Brady, *Magic Weapons: China's Political Influence Activities under Xi Jinping*, Conference paper presented at the conference on "The corrosion of democracy under China's global influence," Arlington, Virginia, USA, September 16-17, 2017, Wilson Center, 2017, p. 9.

[12] G. Sapelli, *Oltre il capitalismo. Macchine, lavoro, proprietà*, Milano, Guerini e Associati, 2018.

[13] D. Shambaugh, "China's propaganda system: Institutions, processes and efficacy," *The China Journal*, 57, 2007, pp. 25- 58.

¹⁴ A.-M. Brady, "China's propaganda machine," Wilson Center, 26/10/2015, www.wilsoncenter.org.
¹⁵ Ibid.
¹⁶ S. Jiang, "Beijing has a new propaganda weapon: Voice of China," *CNN.com*, 21/3/2018, money.cnn.com.
¹⁷ Reports without Borders for Freedom of Information, *2018 World Press Freedom Index*, rsf.org; Freedom House, *Freedom of the Press 2017. Press Freedom's Dark Horizon*, freedomhouse.org.
¹⁸ "Putin talks NSA, Syria, Iran, drones in RT interview," *Russia Today*, 12/6/2013, www.rt.com.
¹⁹ T.C. Helmus *et al.*, *Russian Social Media Influence*, Rand, 2018, p. 11.
²⁰ D. McGuinness, "Russia steps into Berlin 'rape' storm claiming German cover-up," *BBC News*, 27/1/2016, www.bbc.com.
²¹ T.C. Helmus *et al.*, *Russian Social Media Influence*, cit., pp. 12–13.
²² A. Chen, "What Mueller's indictment reveals about Russia's Internet Research Agency," *New Yorker*, 16/2/2018, www.newyorker.com.
²³ A. Chen, "The Agency," *New York Times*, 6/6/2015.
²⁴ See the declarations of the marketing and communication expert Kip Knight: F. Bechis, "Vi spiego come e perché Isis e russi sono maestri di fake news. Parola di Kip Knight," *Formiche.net*, 22/10/2017, www. formiche.net.
²⁵ E. Rossi, "Us Really, ecco come la guerra della disinformazione russa prosegue," *Formiche.net*, 13/7/2018, www.formiche.net.
²⁶ For the analysis by FireEye see FireEye Intelligence, "Suspected Iranian influence operation leverages network of inauthentic news sites & social media targeting audiences in US, UK, Latin America, Middle East," 21/8/2018, www.fireeye.com.
²⁷ A. Hern, "Russian hackers targeting conservative US 28 thinktanks, Microsoft says," *The Guardian*, 21/8/2018.
²⁸ B. O'Brien, C. Bing, "Russian hackers targeted U.S Senate, think tanks: Microsoft," *Reuters*, 21/8/2018, www.reuters.com.
²⁹ Ibid.
³⁰ J. Barnes, M. Rosenberg, "Kremlin sources go quiet, leaving C.I.A. in the dark about Putin's plans for midterms," *New York Times*, 24/8/2018.
³¹ F. Bechis, "Il Cremlino, le interferenze, e quella chiamata per compromettere la Nato. Parla Paolo Alli," 19/2/2018, *Formiche.net*, 13/7/2018, www.formiche.net.
³² S. Walker, "Kremlin calling? Meet the Russian pranksters who say 'Elton owes us,'" *The Guardian*, 13/3/2016, www.theguardian.com.
³³ Five, to be specific: Sahar, Al-Kawthar, Al-Alam, Qods TV and Press TV: M. Torfeh, "The role of Iran's regional media in its soft war policy," *Al Jazeera.net*, 16/2/2017, http://studies.aljazeera.net.
³⁴ This is the former IRGC commander Ezatollah Zarghami, director of the IRIB from 2004 to 2014: M.F. Wehrey *et al.*, *The Rise of the Pasdaran: Assessing the Domestic Roles of Iran's Islamic Revolutionary Guards Corps*, Vol. 821, Rand Corporation, 2009, p. 50.
³⁵ C. Walker et. al., «Authoritarianism goes global», *The American Interest*, 28.3.2016, www.the-american-interest.com.
³⁶ International Campaign for Human Rights in Iran, *Iran's State TV: A Major Human Rights Violator*, IRIB Briefing Paper, June 2014, www.iranhumanrights.org.
³⁷ S. Kamali Denghan, «Trump plans to enforce sanctions against Iran state TV, says source», *The Guardian*, 8.1.2018, www.theguardian.com.

[38] «Chinese FDI squeezed in 2017 by regulatory crackdowns at home and abroad», Baker McKenzie, 17.1.2018, www.bakermckenzie.com.

[39.] K. Jayaram, *The Closest Look Yet at Chinese Economic Engagement in Africa*, Mc Kinsey & Company, June 2018, www.mckinsey.com.

[40] A.-M. Brady, *Magic Weapons*, cit., p. 10.

[41] G. Kanwal, *Pakistan's Gwadar Port: A New Naval Base in China's String of Pearls in the Indo-Pacific*, CSIS, 2.4.2018, www.csis.org.

[42] A. Wilts, «US must 'prepare' for possible war with China, admiral warns», *The Independent*, 15.2.2018, www.independent.co.uk.

[43] D. Thorne, B. Spevack, *Harbored Ambition. How China's Port Investments Are Strategically reshaping the Indo-Pacific*, C4ADS, 2017.

[44] European Parliament Think Tank, *Energy as a Tool of Foreign Policy of Authoritarian States, in Particular Russia*, 27.4.2018, http://www.europarl.europa.eu.

[45] Fra le aziende che collaborano con Gazprom ci sono la francese ENGIE, l'austriaca OMV, le tedesche Wintershall e Uniper, l'olandese Shell.

4   Where the Battle is Fought, in Cyberspace

If 20 years ago you had gone to the army's national selection and recruitment center with your resume and asked to be enrolled in a cyber unit, the official on duty would probably have peered at you with inquiring eyes, with a mix of astonishment and irritation. Today you could take your pick. Politicians, military personnel and experts now consider cyberspace as an established reality, a new domain of warfare equal to land, air, sea and space. All of the armies of developed countries, although with very different degrees of expertise and know-how, have a unit dedicated to cyberwarfare that operates alongside the army, the navy or the air force. The cyber dimension has entered by right into military doctrine, the documents of international organizations and immediately into the private sector, that has begun to invest in cybersecurity to prevent hidden threats on the Internet and protect sensitive data from incursions by hacker collectives.

To give some substance to a term that still has difficulty entering common language, we can imagine cyberspace as a three-dimensional reality. A first level consists of the hardware, i.e. the sum of the physical components that constitute its base: computers, cables, processors, hard disks and so forth. The second level consists of all of the cyber operators, i.e. the individuals that are active in cyberspace. As with electronic components, they are also subject to the laws and policies of the state in which they are located. Software, which experts also call the "logical network" (in contrast to the "physical network" of the hardware), can be considered as the third part of cyberspace and constitutes the sum of the information and data that flow uninterrupted on the Internet. Reclaiming state sovereignty on this part of cyberspace is an operation that presents more than one problem, yet various states consider software the same as a territory over which to exercise their sovereignty.

After making the necessary distinctions, it is useful to understand what the implications of cyberwarfare are, and what happens when these instruments end up in the wrong hands. Although most cyber attacks are traceable to collectives or organizations that do not have official links with state entities, here we will try to discover why cyberwarfare is one of the most effective instruments with which a state can exert its sharp power and hit the enemy's infrastructure, data and security. When we speak of the cyber universe the distinction between democratic and illiberal states no longer applies. All developed states have established military and civilian cyber units and invest money in research. Nor does the distinction between offensive and defensive use of cyber instruments hold up, because each state that wishes to guarantee its own security must be ready to consider both alternatives. Although international law is gravely behind in codifying the subject, there is by now a consolidated conviction that a cyber attack by an organization sponsored by a state is to be considered an open act of military aggression.

Already in the Pentagon's first cybersecurity strategy, in 2011, it states that an attack by a collective affiliated with a state can constitute an act of war and require the use of military force in response.[1] NATO itself has officially reinterpreted Article 5 of the Collective Defense Treaty. At the end of the NATO summit in Wales of September 2014, the heads of state and government of the member countries set down the new doctrine in black and white, writing in the joint declaration that "Cyber attacks can reach a threshold that threatens national and Euro-Atlantic prosperity, security, and stability" and that as a consequence "cyber defence is part of NATO's core task of collective defence."[2] The European Union has followed the same path, beginning to give more importance to cybersecurity despite having to deal with mutual vetoes from member countries within the European Council. It is clear at this point that we are faced with a global trend, where the cyber dimension is unanimously considered a new frontier with the most diverse applications.

> Everyone uses a computer for reasons of necessity, habit or mere convenience. Internet has created a new dimension that has greatly changed both the military and the civilian world. It is necessary to decide what use to make of these cyber instruments in times of peace and of war, and anticipate what their side

effects can be – explains Edward Luttwak, a military strategy expert and political analyst, formerly a member of the Pentagon National Security Study Group.[3]

There are not good states and bad states. The cyber universe entails both defensive and offensive use of these resources, the shield and the sword. Those who don't already have one, are now working to establish a cyber command. An artillery corps does not produce great economic advances except in sectors such as the iron and steel industry. A cyber unit can cause great harm if it is poorly designed, but if it is done intelligently, it can become an important tool for national education. Consider the state of Israel, that years ago established cyber unit 8200, the single largest unit in the army. Those who are able to pass the aptitude test at 18 years of age, with or without a diploma, become part of the unit, where for five years they undergo infantry training and cyber preparation. Once the course is over some of these kids remain in the army, but most of them create their own businesses in the sector and provide an enormous contribution to the national economy. This is one of the reasons that Israel has become an unrivaled cyber power.

Cyberwarfare: nobody is safe

Alongside the use of cyber instruments for civilian purposes, in recent years we have seen growing assertiveness by states, state-controlled organizations or even lone wolves that operate in the cyber domain to intimidate, threaten and attack the enemy. Cyberwarfare has taken on dimensions such as to require a rethinking of the defense system of states and a diversion of funds for intelligence to organizations dedicated to cybersecurity.

There are various ways a state or a criminal organization can operate in the cyber domain to strike an enemy or pursue a political agenda. We have already seen the potential of cyberpropaganda campaigns channeled through the use of bots, the creation of fake social network accounts or the hacking of real ones. As dangerous as these operations are, they are only the tip of the iceberg. Other instruments can cause much more serious and immediate damage. One of them is doxing, the term experts use to identify the practice of taking private information and making it public with the specific aim of embarrassing the targeted subject (this is the goal of the Wikileaks organization created by Julian Assange). Then there is the use of malware to spy on the enemy and attack its sensitive infrastructure.

This practice is preferred by authoritarian states, that know they can act with a low possibility of being traced, but is also not eschewed by democratic states: EternalBlue, one of the best-known operations in the hacker world, was designed by the United States National Security Agency (NSA) and then stolen and made public in April 2017 by a hacker collective known by the name The Shadow Brokers.[4] According to experts, the NSA, along with Israeli intelligence, was also the author of Stuxnet, the virus that repeatedly struck the Iranian nuclear plants and deactivated their centrifuges, first under the Bush Administration, and then with Obama in the White House.[5]

Attacks of this scale, prepared directly by intelligence agencies, are certainly not daily occurrences, Most acts of aggression against the national security of another country are carried out by hacker collectives or organized groups sponsored by a government or at least affiliated with one. Illiberal countries like Russia, China and North Korea have made this type of offensive routine. The difficulty in tracing cybercrimes perpetrated by criminal organizations directly to state actors makes it particularly inviting for these states to use hacker collectives. This creates numerous complications for the cybersecurity structures of the states under attack, as stressed in an interview Formiche published with General John Allen, former commander of NATO's International Security Assisyance Force (ISAF) mission in Afghanistan, and currently president of the Brookings Institution:

> It's hard to tell, whether it's State, non-State or criminal actors. The entity that is engaging in the cyber domain may be doing so at one particular moment to undertake cybercrime, that same entity might be engaging in activities in the cyberdomain for the purpose of cyberterrorism and later could be engaging in the cyberdomain for the purpose of cyberwarfare. For this reason it's very hard to deter this kind of activities in the cyber environment.
> Forensics associated with attribution are difficult. The North Korean organization known as Unit 181, which calls itself Lazarus, emptied a bank account stealing 80 million dollars and the same Unit was the source of the ransomware Wannacry. Petya was a huge blow against the Ukrainians and there's the theory out there that Petya was a test-virus to test the potential they may use against the United States and their allies.[6]

Along with technological innovation, there has also been an increase in the methodical way some states use cyberwarfare to subvert the international order, inject doubts and divisions in unwanted strategic alliances, steal sensitive information to strike their enemies at their weakest points, and expose their plans to the public. According to Edward Luttwak, there are no doubts about the links of criminal organizations now known to the general public such as the Russian hacker collective Fancy Bear or the North Korean group APT37 (Advanced Persistent Threat) to their respective governments.

> They are military units of the state. The Russians are the best at this because Russia is a country with a strong mathematical culture. The Iranians have been active for a while, but they are far behind because the cultural level in the Middle East on cyber questions is still mediocre. North Korea often uses these units to attack other states, although it is a limited phenomenon. They succeeded in penetrating Sony's systems in California in 2014, but North Korean hackers have limited capabilities.

The case of China is different, as we will see in more detail later. Experts speak of an army of tens of thousands men payed by the government.[7]

> In China these hackers may even work in an office in Shanghai – continues the American political analyst – working days and nights in buildings in the center of the city, and they may walk down the streets dressed as civilians, but they remain military personnel.

The tactics, resources and goals of cyberwarfare can change considerably from one country to another depending on the historical background and political agenda pursued by the respective governments. In this chapter we will briefly trace the evolution of cyberwarfare as an instrument of sharp power.

The Russian Bear and cyberwarfare: a successful marriage

In Moscow one rarely hears talk of cyberwarfare (*kibervoyna*). The Russians prefer to use the term *information warfare* or refer to "special operations" (*spetsoperatsii*), and that is no coincidence. In the Russian narrative these names are almost always used to expose or condemn presumed Western interference in their internal affairs. The cyber aspect is only one element of a grand strategy pursued by the Kremlin since the start of the Cold War. Disinformation campaigns, espionage and cyber operations are all manifestations of that *informatsionnaya voyna* to which the Gerasimov doctrine refers directly, when the general states that "The information space opens wide asymmetrical possibilities for reducing the fighting potential of the enemy."[8]

In recent years, and specifically after the Russian invasion of Crimea, the Western media began to indicate the Russian war strategies with the name of "hybrid warfare," a term that has taken its place in the strategic documents of NATO and other international organizations. According to this current the hybrid nature of Russian warfare lies in the joint use of instruments of psychological warfare, trolls, economic warfare and sabotage of electoral systems, assisted by conventional military operations. The truth is that hybrid warfare is nothing new. The United States war in Vietnam, the war between the Soviet Union and the Afghan rebels, or the conflict between Israel and Hezbollah were all classified as "hybrid wars" because they were fought with a broad range of instruments (espionage, guerrilla warfare, the use of regular troops and contractors). The evolution of Russian hybrid warfare should thus not be sought in a new doctrinal approach but more in the possibility to use new technologies and thus expand the range of military operations. As Keir Giles has written,

> Despite Russian doctrinal references to indirect and asymmetric methods, hybridity does not define the totality of the new Russian way of war. The role of conventional and asymmetric tools and capabilities in Russian military thinking and doctrine has to be placed in the context of Moscow's perceived overall strategic challenges, in which major conventional and nuclear conflict loom large.[9]

It is true, however, that under the leadership of Vladimir Putin, the Kremlin has gradually institutionalized cyberwarfare, inaugurating specific military units. Despite the long-term experience of the Russian government in the field of information operations (IO), the Russian armed forces have only recently embraced the cause of cyberwarfare, that was once the exclusive prerogative of agencies controlled by services such as the Federal Security Service of the Russian Federation (FSB), the Main Intelligence Directorate (GRU) or the Foreign Intelligence Service (SVR).[10]

An initial proving ground to test Russia's offensive capability in the cyber domain presented itself in Estonia in May 2007, when a large-scale cyber attack hit the servers of the government, banks, the principal media channels and critical infrastructure, knocking them out for almost a month. Although it was never proven that the Russian government was involved, the sense of timing and coordination of the operation left little doubt. The casus belli, experts believe, was the removal of a bronze statue of a Soviet soldier located in the center of Tallinn that recalled the liberation of Estonia from the Nazis by Russia. The gesture had provoked indignation and violent protests by the Russian-speaking population in Estonia, as well as a harsh diplomatic condemnation from the Kremlin. The cyber campaign against the Tallinn government had limited practical effects, but reached its goal: destabilize a country in full transition towards the West, Europe and NATO. The psychological impact was significant, in part because Estonia has always boasted of a level of digitalization and access to Internet unrivalled on the Old Continent.

No less important were the consequences of the coordinated cyber attacks against the government of Georgia during the war with Russia in the summer of 2008. The invasion of Georgia by the Russian army, navy and air force, launched immediately after the intervention of the Georgian armed forces in South Ossetia, was preceded by a DDoS attack (distributed denial of service) against government servers and some transport and telecommunications companies. In this case as well, it was not possible to trace the offensive directly to the Russian government, that for its part denied any involvement and suggested it could have been the work of lone wolves. However the scope, timing and resources involved indicated an unusual level of coordination for a criminal organization. The suspicion that cyber attacks against the government served to pave the way for a subsequent military intervention was fueled in particular by a certain geographic alignment of the moves of the Russian army. This was the case of the hacker attack against the government sites in Gori, a small city in the East of Georgia, perpetrated a few hours prior to a bombardment by the Russian air force.[11]

The cyber offensives in Estonia and Georgia received considerable international attention, but they still had a limited impact, as they were mostly attacks in the form of DDoS or Structured Query Language (SQL) injections (that target data management applications). An entirely different level was reached with the attacks by Russian hacker collectives against the Ukrainian government that were repeated without interruption from the time of the Maidan square protests through the entire conflict in the Donbas. Although the Russian government has always denied any involvement in the cyber campaign that targeted Ukraine in recent years, experts are almost unanimous in believing these attacks originated in Russia. During the conflict in Crimea, and even after the signing of the Minsk agreements, a full-scale cyber offensive was carried out without interruption against the Kiev government, that was subject to incursions against infrastructure, telecommunications and army facilities. At the beginning it seemed to involve spurious actions, sabotage, malware, and spear phishing, especially close to events with great media visibility such as the Maidan protests or the parliamentary elections in Ukraine in October 2014. In December 2015, the cyberwarfare against Kiev turned a page: in the afternoon of December 23, three of the country's main electricity companies suffered a cyber attack that caused the blackout of their power plants, leaving more than 220,000 people in the dark for six hours during the stiff Ukrainian winter. It was not an impromptu action but an operation prepared for months down to the smallest details, thanks to the acquisition of plant operator credentials that allowed the criminals to operate remotely.[12] After stealing the data to access the plant monitoring system (SCADA) through a Trojan the experts renamed BlackEnergy, the hackers replaced the firmware of the plant control system with a malicious firmware that allowed them to deactivate the electricity supply.[13] Upon completing the operation the operating systems were taken out using a malware, Kill Disk, that blacked out the plant servers and destroyed their data. The Ukrainian intelligences services identified as the responsible party the Russian hacker collective Sandworm, that had already been active for several months in actions of sabotage against the government of Petro Poroshenko. The same conclusions were reached by some of the most important companies in the cybersecurity field. According to the American company iSIGHT Partners, although there was no proof of direct connections with the Kremlin, it was undoubtedly "a Russian actor operating with alignment to the interest of the state."[14] In addition to adding fuel to the flames between Moscow and Kiev, the hit against the Ukrainian power plants opened the door to a new frontier of cyberwarfare. It demonstrated that attacks on the critical infrastructure of a country are not only able to cause serious economic harm, but have a psychological impact on the population that undermines trust in the institutions' ability to defend their citizens. In the case of the BlackEnergy malware of December 2015, the experts were unanimous in finding that if the attackers had wanted to, they could have definitively knocked out the power plants. The true aim of the blackout was not so much the physical destruction of the operating systems as it was to launch a message to the Ukrainian population: the institutions are not able to protect you, your infrastructure is not reliable.

The attacks we have presented as examples have a common characteristic: they were planned in detail and executed by hacker collectives equipped with resources, expertise and organization beyond the reach of a private citizen, and acted in full respect for the Russian political agenda against countries considered to be enemies of the Russian Federation.

Some of these teams of hackers answer directly to the Russian government, while others to some oligarchs that act on their own. There is more than one good reason to rely on these units: they cost relatively little, they can be activated rapidly and if necessary disbanded from one day to the next, they guarantee anonymity and they can easily disappear.[15] Diversions do not always work, though. Less sensational than the interference in the US presidential elections, but just as serious, is the case of the cyberattack by some authors with a Russian IP address who in March of 2016 struck (and partially blacked out) nine information websites in Sweden. It was only in the summer of 2018, after the declassification of a US State Department document picked up by Buzzfeed News, that the news brought the danger of Russian government interference into Sweden's public policy to the center of the country's political debate. The timing of the attacks was once again the clue that drew the attention of American intelligence. While the Swedish newspapers had to deal with the blackout of their servers for five days, the Swedish Parliament was discussing the appropriateness of a collaboration agreement with NATO.[16] The agreement, that was signed the following May, marked a fundamental step in a long approach between Sweden and the Atlantic Alliance for which the Russian government never hid its disdain.[17]

In the much better known case of the hacking of the Democratic National Committee (DNC) in March 2016, the two Russian units that stole the e-mails and data of more than half a million voters from the Democrats to create problems for Hillary Clinton were also unable to cancel the tracks of their actions. The two groups involved in the computer attack on the political committee, known in the intelligence community by the names Cozy Bear and Fancy Bear, were identified as units affiliated with the Russian intelligence services. These were the conclusions reached not only by various leading global firms in the cybersecurity sector such as FireEye or CrowdStrike, but also the investigations led by Special Prosecutor Robert Mueller on the case, that came into the news with the name of Russiagate. On July 13, 2018, the former FBI Director in charge of the investigations indicted 12 Russian GRU agents with the accusation of having conspired to "to gain unauthorized access (to 'hack') into the computers of US persons and entities involved in the 2016 US presidential election, steal from those computers, and stage releases of the stolen documents to interfere with the 2016 US presidential election."[18]

Cozy Bear and Fancy Bear, already known in the intelligence world under other names (Cozy Car and Sofacy, or more simply APT28 and APT29), had already scored various cyber incursions before hitting Hillary Clinton's election campaign. The rich record of the two Russian hacker groups already included hits against the Pentagon, the White House, and a long list of cyber attacks against institutions and infrastructure of European countries. Never before had the investigations succeeded in tracing the smoking gun to one of the many service agencies that work for the Russian government, often one against the other.[19] Thus the indictment of the 12 GRU agents by Mueller, regardless of the conclusion of the investigations, marks a break with the past and removes any alibi for the Kremlin, that can no longer speak of "lone wolves" to justify interference in the 2016 presidential elections.

Glasses, coat and tie: the cyber face of the Dragon

As we have discussed for Russian cyberwarfare, to understand the importance of the cyber domain for the Chinese government and army we need to first make a point regarding method. The definition of cyber that we usually find in reconstructions by the media and Western experts, i.e. that of a domain limited to the Internet and the world of electronics, is not the same to which Chinese media, government agencies and experts refer.

Exactly like the Russians, the Chinese consider the cyber domain as part of a broader framework: the information space, that is, the sum of information which citizens can access through the Internet, media and oral communication. Likewise, in China the term "cyberwarfare" is used exclusively with reference to cyber operations by Western states. The Chinese prefer to speak of information warfare, a frontier that includes both offensive cyber operations by the People's Liberation Army (PLA) and the government agencies under its control, and the censure and constant control of the internal information space. The holistic approach the Chinese take to cyberwarfare, that explains the dirigistic management of media and the web by the state, as well as a certain lexical incompatibility with the West, has made it difficult to reach a common international coding of the subject-matter. Under a liberal, multi-stakeholder vision, proposed in international conventions by Western states, the Chinese government, that sees uncontrolled information as a danger and not an opportunity, has always defended a primary role for nation-states in controlling their cyberspace; this view is shared by Russia and other Central Asian states. It is not rare for the difference in views to lead to a stalemate, with two opposing factions in the General Assembly of the United Nations, consisting of the United States and European countries on one side, and the states of the Shanghai Cooperation Organization (SCO) on the other.[20] The apple of discord is not only an opposing view of international law, but also a different conception of freedom of navigators: in Chinese political culture maintaining social order is more important than citizens' privacy and freedom of thought.

What makes it difficult to fully understand Chinese cyberstrategy is the absence of a consolidated doctrine. In only the last few years, and specifically with the presidency of Xi Jinping, the Chinese government has come out into the open and launched a process of institutionalization of cyberwarfare, creating new civilian and military organizations and increasing investments in cyber research. One of the first documents that outlines a Chinese cyber strategy is a book from the end of the nineties that had aroused a great deal of interest abroad: *Unrestricted Warfare*, written by Qiao Lang and Wang Xiangsui, two pillars of the Chinese army.[21] The book, improperly interpreted by Western media as an instruction manual to attack and destroy the United States, explains how a country such as China can confront and overpower a technologically superior country through the use of asymmetrical instruments such as sabotage of enemy networks without resorting to the use of traditional military strength (which would mark its defeat). Twenty years ago that book opened up a lively debate, puncturing a myth that still endures in the media narrative today (especially in Chinese media), positing that the military, economic and cultural growth of China is dictated only by a view of win-win cooperation with its global competitors.

Rather, the truth is that competition with Western powers, with the United States at the top of the list, has been a fundamental driver for technological innovation and the modernization of the army. Conscious of their inability to compete at Washington's level in the military field (although the gap has now been considerably reduced), China decided to invest in the cyber domain, where it believes it is second to none in the world today. According to the experts, a series of regional crises that involved China in the nineties raised an alarm in Beijing, laying bare the gaps in the Dragon's military preparedness compared to the United States.[22] This was true, for example, in the case of the third Taiwan Strait Crisis, when in 1996, faced with Beijing's threat to bomb the island, Bill Clinton deployed the largest American military fleet in Asia since the Vietnam War to defend its ally, forcing the Chinese government to back off. The recognition of the military gap with the United States pushed the Chinese government of the time to start a process of modernization of the PLA and to invest in new weapons designed with the specific aim of hitting the Unite States' weak spots. This has remained a constant in the Dragon's military (and cyber) strategy documents. When it is not possible to reach the adversary due to insufficiency of resources and know-how, it is best to shift course and invest time and money to beat the competitor where he is weakest. This philosophy was expressed by President Jiang Zemin, who was responsible for a radical reform of the army at the beginning of the 2000s, in a celebrated phrase: "that which the enemy fears most, that is what we must develop."[23]

In recent decades various bodies, such as the State Council of Information Office (SCIO) or specific working groups established by the Politburo, have drawn up programmatic documents for a Chinese cyber security strategy. One example is Document 27, a national security strategy drawn up in 2003 by the State Network and Information Security Coordination Small Group, presided over then by Prime Minister Li Keqiang[24]; or the national program for medium to long-term development of science and technology, an SCIO document considered by experts to be a benchmark of the Dragon's cybersecurity strategy. An initial attempt by the party to find a unitary strategy for the cyber dimension and information control took place with the establishment of the Small Leading Group for Internet Security and Informatization in February 2014.[25] Presided over by Xi Jinping in person, an unprecedented situation in the history of the party, the working group was born of the need to bring two equally important tasks under joint control: IT security and information control, "two wings of one bird, two wheels on one car," to use a well-known definition given by Xi.[26] The impulse given by Xi's presidency has only in part resolved the institutional fragmentation that has always characterized Chinese cybergovernance. Today there are dozens of government agencies and army departments that deal with every dimension of the cyber domain; from those that work on web censure to those that deal with the security of critical infrastructure, to units dedicated to cyberwarfare. We will concentrate here above all on the latter, to understand the importance for the efficacy of Chinese sharp power of the activities of the army and hacker organizations not directly traceable to the government.

The all-inclusive reform of the army launched in 2015 by Xi Jinping marked the opening of a new era for the Dragon's cyberwarfare, implementing the directives set out in the white paper on Chinese military strategy published in 2015, which stated that the Chinese armed forces were to "build a logistics system that can provide support for fighting and winning modern wars, serve the modernization of the armed forces, and transform towards informatization."[27] After having placed the navy, the air force and the missile division on the same level as the army for the first time, a necessary condition to face the joint military operations that characterize modern warfare, a new division was introduced, the Strategic Support Force (SSF), with the double goal of presiding over operations in space (launch and control of satellites, interference with signals of other satellites, etc.) and in cyberspace (cyberwarfare, electronic warfare). Although various doubts remain regarding the functioning of this division (for example, it is not clear if it reports directly to the Central Military Commission, as other divisions do), its introduction brought the entire army and Chinese military doctrine into the era of information warfare once and for all, reducing the historical gap with Western powers.

It is plausible that in the near future, the SSF could take control of most cyber operations. For the moment, the Chinese army seems to have kept the old units dedicated to cyberwarfare. In recent years, the Third Department (3/PLA), a sort of counterpart of the US NSA, has received particular media attention for having conducted cyber operations abroad. Located in Beijing, the department is divided into 12 bureaus, each with a different function: from satellite communication to intelligence analysis to surveillance of individuals. Two of these operational bureaus, the second and the twelfth, merit particular attention. Known to the intelligence community (and also to the general public by now) with the names of Unit

61398 and Unit 61486, these two units based in Shanghai are among the most lethal Chinese cyber actors. The first division came to the public's attention in 2013 thanks to a report by the cybersecurity company Mandiant.[28] Expert investigations, confirmed by intelligence sources and widely reported on in the international press, have traced a long trail of cyber attacks against the institutions and critical infrastructure of the United States beginning in 2006, from the Pentagon to the State Department to giants such as Coca-Cola, to this unit based in Shanghai.[29] The report, firmly denied by the Chinese government, concluded that hundreds or even thousands of employees could work in the second bureau.[30] The twelfth bureau, known among experts with the name of Putter Panda, is just as dangerous. According to the cybersecurity company CrowdStrike, the PLA office has carried out cyber attacks against European and American companies operating in the defense and aerospace sectors.[31]

What we have presented to this point helps understand the level of institutionalization that Chinese cyberwarfare has acquired over the years, although only on a superficial level. As Luttwak recalls, most cyber attacks originating from Russia and China are directed by state employees, officials or military personnel, and not by "somebody sitting on their bed that weighs 400 pounds," the colorful expression used by President Trump in speaking of responsibility for interference in the 2016 presidential elections.[32] This does not mean that hacker collectives that operate on their own do not exist in China, without having to report to the government. Just as in Russia, China also has dozens of groups of cybercriminals engaged in espionage and data theft on the web. It is not simple to connect the Chinese government to the activity of collectives such as the Red Hacker Alliance, an organization that has been active since the start of the 2000s, which has hundreds of members.[33] Sometimes these people act with their own means and goals, driven by nationalist aims, or more rarely, by profit. The Chinese government is aware of the existence of these "patriotic" hackers, and often finds itself in a bind: open support risks triggering a bilateral clash with the targeted countries, while ignoring their requests or even distancing themselves can mean setting these extremely dangerous actors against them. The proliferation of these groups that intend to fully pursue Beijing's political agenda, even causing difficulties for the party leadership, is the paradoxical price to pay for a country that has always used nationalist rhetoric, although always veiled in constant calls for cooperation, to justify investments in technological research, modernization of the army and cyberwarfare. By now it is evident that the goal is no longer catch-up, but to obtain the same military capabilities as a superpower like the United States. The drive for technological modernization of the armed forces and the institutionalization of new units dedicated to cyberoffense is rather based on the idea, indicated in Chinese military strategy and civilian documents as well, of *Sha Shou Jian* ("the assassin's club")[34]: if you obtain the right resources, one way or the other, you can defeat an enemy that is much larger and stronger than you.

Iran: the last to arrive (not to be underestimated)

With respect to states such as Russia, China, the United States and Israel, Iran is a latecomer to cyberwarfare. Until just a few years ago the Islamic Republic was considered a second-rate cyber power. The relative scarcity of resources, together with a limited budget and a fragmented organization left the Iranian government on the fringe of the battle for supremacy in the cyber domain for a long time. Today things have changed. The media clamor provoked in America by the Russiagate case has diverted the attention of the international media away from cyberwarfare directed by Teheran. This is an egregious error of evaluation. While the scandal of Russian interference raged, US intelligence and private cybersecurity companies observed an increase in cyber activity by Iranian actors linked to the government of Hassan Rouhani.

Before briefly retracing the Iranian cyberstory it is necessary to once again state a premise: if Iran has decided to embrace the cause of cyber war, it is because it has often been a victim of cyber incursions by foreign states in the past. The Stuxnet attack, which we have already cited, in which American and Israeli intelligence struck at the Iranian nuclear plant of Natanz, deactivating more than 1,000 centrifuges, set Iran's nuclear progress back a year, and is still an open wound for Teheran. The fear, which is not groundless, of an imminent attempt at regime change directed by Western powers through the Internet has pushed the Iranian government to tighten its grip on the web over the years, making censure of contents more sophisticated and silencing the sirens from abroad that called the opposition to action against the regime.

A first testing ground that forced the Iranian government to unleash its cyber militias, according a detailed Carnegie report, was the wave of protests that overwhelmed the institutions of Teheran after the re-election of Mahmoud Ahmadinejad in June 2009.[35] While Congress and the US Administration, then led by Barack Obama, asked the managers of social networks to keep access open to their platforms for political dissidents, a hacker collective that dubbed itself the Iranian Cyber Army (ICA) began to attack the web sites of the principal opposition movements, blacking them out through malware or DDoS attacks. Over time, surveillance and the repression of the regime's enemies thanks to the support of hacker units became routine activities. The ICA is only one of the many hacker groups now active in Iranian cyberspace. This collective's contacts with the Teheran government and the army are hard to prove, and this makes their activity particularly efficient. The simplicity and scarcity of means with which these criminals operate in cyberspace could make it seem they are lone wolves. Yet there are some clues that make it very plausible to suppose if not open support, at least a certain indulgence by the Iranian government in their regard. Like Russian and Chinese hackers, the Iranian organizations also operate by pursuing the political agenda of Ali Khamenei and the government, targeting only countries that are enemies of Iran (the United States, Saudi Arabia and Israel, to cite those at the top of the list) or Iranian dissidents abroad, often with attacks lacking any economic justification. Moreover, and this may be the most revealing aspect, hacker attacks against individuals who are seen negatively by the Iranian government often take place a few days before they are arrested.

A clear example of the coordination between Iranian intelligence and hacker groups was the arrest of Babak Zanjani in December 2013. The Iranian billionaire is the executive director of Sorinet Group, one of the largest industrial conglomerates in the country. The company, which is based in the United Arab Emirates, has already been in the crosshairs of US intelligence for having helped Iran evade sanctions. Zanjani was arrested by the Iranian police with the accusation of corruption, and subsequently sentenced to death (as of this writing the sentence has not yet been carried out).[36] In the weeks prior to the arrest, the iCloud accounts of Zanjani and his employees at Sorinet were repeatedly violated by a group of cybercriminals known with the name of Flying Kitten.[37] Whether or not the hackers were taking orders from the government, one thing is clear: few in Iran believe in coincidences. The Iranian government usually limits itself to tolerating the presence of these actors in cyberspace while denying any responsibility.

Khamenei and Rouhani often point the finger at enemies such as the United States and Israel, spreading conspiratorial rhetoric through state news agencies aimed at uniting the Iranian people against enemy interference. Only in exceptional cases has the government admitted direct involvement in cyber operations. This almost always involved the censure of web sites linked to opposition movements. In December 2013, for example, the Government announced that the Revolutionary Guard had blacked out nine sites of humanitarian organizations accused of having received funding from abroad.[38]

If for the Teheran government online surveillance of dissidents, reformist politicians and high-level officials is a daily activity, cyberwar abroad presents multiple problems. Attacks against the sites of government agencies or ministries of large powers are still beyond the range of Iranian hackers, who prefer to target non-governmental organizations or companies in the defense and energy sectors. The United States has often ended up in the crosshairs of Iranian hackers, who can boast some success out of the dozens of moderate attacks carried out. Between 2011 and 2013 a group of Iranian cybercriminals known to intelligence services with the name of Izz ad-Din al-Qassam Cyber Fighters launched a DDoS attack against the servers of 50 US financial institutions, including the New York Stock Exchange and JPMorgan Chase. By putting the targeted servers out of commission, "Operation Ababil" blocked thousands of bank accounts and is still today considered the most devastating Iranian hacker attack on United States soil.[39] The FBI investigations concluded with the indictment of seven "individuals employed by two Iran-based computer companies sponsored and directed by the Iranian government."[40]

Most of Iranian cyberwarfare is directed against its historical regional enemies. Saudi Arabia occupies the top spot in the thoughts of Iranian hackers. The two countries have always been ferocious enemies, divided by faith and ethnicity (the Saudis are Sunni and Arab, the Iranians Shiite and Persians), lined up against each other in Yemen, Lebanon, Syria and Iraq; for some time now, Iran and Saudi Arabia have opened a new cyber front to consolidate their sharp power in the Middle East. When it is not possible to respond directly to presumed cyber aggressions by the United States or Israel, due to an evident difference in capacity, the Iranians take aim at an ally of those countries, Saudi Arabia, that on multiple occasions has shown an inability to defend itself. Among the Iranian attacks that have hurt the government of Riyadh the most we should recall the sabotage in 2012 of tens of thousands of computers of Saudi Aramco, the flagship company of the Saudi government and global leader in the oil sector. Insult was added to the economic injury, when the computer hard drives were filled with images of American flags in flames. It caused great embarrassment to the Saudi monarchy. In the subsequent years Iranian hackers hit the institutions, businesses and foundations of Saudi Arabia almost without interruption. It is no coincidence that Saudi Foreign Minister Adel al-Jubeir recently defined the Islamic Republic of Iran the "most dangerous nation behind cyber attacks."[41]

The remark by the Saudi Minister is dictated by political logic, but contains an element of truth. It is true that Iran cannot boast the same technology as cyber superpowers such as Russia, China, the United States and Israel. The organizational fragmentation in the government that often leads to clashes between the Revolutionary Guard, the political leadership and the religious leadership undermines the basis for efficiency of state cyberwarfare. The mass exodus of students, scientists and engineers does not help, which has afflicted the country's economy for years, depriving it of many outstanding individuals. Despite this, the growing activity of Iranian cybercriminals recently detected by intelligence agencies and private companies must not be underestimated. Some of the most active Persian hacker collectives in the Middle East have begun to turn their attention to the West. The Trump Administration's escalation towards the Rouhani government after the US withdrawal from the nuclear agreement (Joint Comprehensive Plan of Action) led to the start of a new wave of cyber attacks of Iranian origin. US intelligence has focused its attention on a series of collectives that have recently resumed attacking the country[42]: Rocket Kitten has a preference for espionage and data theft from companies in the defense sector; OilRig, one of the most active Iranian hacker groups in Saudi Arabia, is now a frequent visitor to the servers of American financial institutions; the collective APT33 uses spear fishing to target e-mail accounts of single employees of companies in the energy and aviation sectors.[43] Cyber crime, which until a few years ago was used by Iranian police forces to keep order and repress internal dissent, is now a weapon in the hands of the myriad of hacker collectives that follow the political agenda of the ayatollahs with military discipline, and a fundamental driver for Iranian sharp power in the region. The rise of the Islamic Republic to the big leagues of cyber superpowers has only been postponed.

Notes

[1] US Department of Defense, *Department of Defense Strategy for Operating in Cyberspace*, July 2011, csrc.nist.gov.
[2] NATO, *Wales Summit Declaration Issued by the Heads of State and Government Participating in the meeting of the North Atlantic Council in Wales*, 26/9/2016, www.nato.int.
[3] Exclusive interview for this book, 11/7/2018.
[4] S. Shane *et al.*, "Security breach and spilled secrets have shaken the N.S.A. to its core," *New York Times*, 12/11/2017, www.nytimes.com.
[5] E. Nakashima, J. Warrick, "Stuxnet was work of US and Israeli experts, officials say," *The Washington Post*, 2/6/2012, www.washingtonpost.com.
[6] F. Bechis, "L'Italia, gli Stati Uniti, la Nato. Intervista esclusiva al generale John Allen," *Formiche.net*, 1/7/2018, www.formiche.net.
[7] M. Hvistendahl, "China's hacker army," *Foreign Policy*, 3/3/2010, foreignpolicy.com.
[8] M.K. McKew, "The Gerasimov Doctrine," *Politico Magazine*, September/October 2017, www.politico.com.
[9] K. Giles, *Russia's "New" Tools for Confronting the West Continuity and Innovation in Moscow's Exercise of Power*, Research Paper, Chatham House, March 2016, www.chathamhouse.org.
[10] M. Connell, S. Vogler, *Russia's Approach to Cyber Warfare*, Center for Naval Analyses Arlington United States, 2017.
[11] "Expert: Cyber-attacks on Georgia websites tied to mob, Russian government," *Los Angeles Times*, 13/8/2008, latimesblogs.latimes.com.
[12] ICS-CERT, *Alert (IR-ALERT-H-16-056-01) Cyber-Attack Against Ukrainian Critical Infrastructure*, original release 25/2/2016, last update 23/8/2018, cs-cert.us-cert.gov.
[13] "Gruppo di continuità," *Wikipedia.it*, last update 24/2/2018, it.wikipedia.org.
[14] J. Finkle, "US firm blames Russian 'Sandworm' hackers for Ukraine outage," *Reuters*, 8/1/2016, www.reuters.com.
[15] M. Connell, S. Vogler, *Russia's approach to Cyber Warfare*, cit.
[16] Atlantic Council, "Sweden ratifies NATO cooperation agreement," *NATOSource*, 25/5/2016, http://www.atlanticcouncil.org.
[17] On July 24, 2018, according to the *Sputnik* web site, Russian Defense Minister Sergei Shoigu threatened to "take measures" in response to the cited collaboration agreement between NATO and the Swedish government: Atlantic Council, "Russia's defense minister threatens response to Sweden and Finland increasing cooperation with NATO," *NATOSource*, 27/8/2018, http://www.atlanticcouncil.org.
[18] *United States of America v. Boris Alekseyevich Antonov et al.*, Case 1:18-cr-00215-ABJ, 13/7/2018, www.justice.gov.
[19] M. Galeotti, *Putin's Hydra: Inside Russia's Intelligence Services*, Policy Brief, European Council on Foreign Relations, May 2016, www.ecfr.eu.
[20] The Shanghai Cooperation Organization (SCO) is an intergovernmental body founded in 1996 by Russia, China, Kazakhstan, Kyrgyzstan and Tajikistan to establish cooperation between the member countries on issues of security, economics and culture. In the subsequent years, Uzbekistan, India and Pakistan also joined.
[21] M. Raud, *China and Cyber: Attitude, Strategies and Organization*, CCDCOE, Tallinn, 2016, p. 9.

22 United States–China Economic and Security Review Commission, *Hearing before the US–China Economic and Security Review Commission One Hundred Fifteenth Congress First Session Thursday, February 23, 2017*, Washington, 2017, www.uscc.gov.
23 A.S. Erickson, T. Heath, "China's turn toward regional restructuring, counter-intervention: A review of authoritative sources," *China Brief*, 15(22), The Jamestown Foundation, 16/11/2015, jamestown.org.
24 Raud, *China and Cyber, cit.*, p. 11.
25 A. Segal, "China's new small leading group on cybersecurity and internet management," *Forbes*, 27/2/2014, www.forbes.com.
26 Raud, *China and Cyber, cit.*, p. 15.
27 The State Council Information Office of the People's Republic of China, *China's Military Strategy (2015)*, May 2015.
28 D. McWhorter, "Mandiant Exposes APT1 – One of China's Cyber Espionage Units & Releases 3,000 Indicators," FireEye, 23/2/2013, www.fireeye.com.
29 "China's army is seen as tied to hacking against U.S," *New York Times*, 18/2/2013, www.nytimes.com.
30 T.P., "Hello, Unit 68," *The Economist*, 19/2/2013, www.economist.com.
31 CrowdStrike, "Hat-tribution to PLA Unit 61486," 9/6/2014, www.crowdstrike.com.
32 E. Weise, "Tech crowd goes wild for Trump's '400-pound hacker,'" *USA Today*, 28/9/2016, eu.usatoday.com.
33 "Red Hacker Alliance," *Wikipedia.en*, last update 12/4/2018, en.wikipedia.org.
34 People's Network, "Dong Feng 21D troop review gives PLA navy an asymmetric 'assassin's mace,'" 9/9/2015.
35 C. Anderson, K. Sadjadpour, *Iran's Cyber Threat: Espionage, Sabotage, and Revenge*, Carnegie Endowment for International Peace, January 2018, carnegieendowment.org.
36 S. Azodi, "Renewed Iran sanctions will bolster the regime and undermine the private sector," *IranSource*, 30/7/2018, http://www.atlanticcouncil.org.
37 C. Anderson, K. Sadjadpour, *Iran's Cyber Threat, cit.*
38 *Ibid.*
39 N. Perlroth, Q. Hardy, "Online banking attacks were work of Iran, US officials say," *New York Times*, 2/1/2013, www.nytimes.com.
40 FBI, "International cyber crime: Iranians charged with hacking US financial sector," 24/3/2016, www.fbi.gov.
41 N. Turak, H. Gamble, "Saudi foreign minister calls Iran most dangerous nation for cyberattacks," *CNBC.com*, 18/2/2018, www.cnbc.com.
42 National Counterintelligence and Security Center, *Foreign Economic Espionage in Cyberspace 2018*, www.dni.gov.
43 FireEye Intelligence, "Advanced persistent threat groups: Who's who of cyber threat actors," www.fireeye.com.

5   The Russian Bear's Tracks in Italy

The Russian connection? It is not an invention from the press to justify the electoral victories of populists like Donald Trump in the United States or the Five Star-League coalition in Italy. Vladimir Putin's moves to transform traditional Russian soft power into a much sharper instrument began as early as 2013; if not before. This was the year in which a Hungarian political analyst, Peter Kreko, published a book with that same title, *The Russian Connection*.[1] The analysis is not dissimilar to that contained in the book written subsequently, in 2015, by Marcel H. Van Herpen, *Putin's Propaganda Machine*.[2] Both analysts describe in detail a particularly effective communications mechanism that makes use of the traditional channels valued in Nye's theory, but adding sophisticated web interference with the use of social networks and supporting information sites. This is a 2.0 version of the propaganda machine deployed on behalf of the then-Soviet Union by the KGB, the secret service Putin comes from. What Kreko wrote in 2013 regarding Russian designs against Europe is striking: "The extremist parties, all anti-EU, will be very useful in this scenario, to weaken the link with the US as well." The uprising in Kiev's Maidan Square had not yet taken place, and the case of the annexation of Crimea and the consequent sanctions imposed by the West had not yet exploded. Putin's plan was already active. The war in Ukraine accelerated and amplified the investments to infiltrate the Old Continent and thus try to realize that Eurasian project, as an alternative to the Euro-Atlantic vision, which seems a lot like redemption after the defeat in the Cold War. To understand the scope of Putin's sharp power towards the outside, there may be no better case to study than that of Italy.

From soft power …

A politically ambitious country like Russia, which claims a sort of "parity" with the United States, cannot not have an official tool of influence towards foreign countries. The Kremlin's political-diplomatic network has the difficult-to-pronounce name of *Rossotrudnichestvo* (Russian Center for Science and Culture). To understand if this is or is not a strategic project fully consistent with the vision of Czar Putin it is sufficient to look at the numbers. In 2013 – a watershed year – the funds for this institution amounted to 48 million euros. In the following years, the amount multiplied, and by 2020 – this is the plan – they will reach 228 million euros.

This organization, which is controlled by the Russian Foreign Ministry and is present in at least 25 countries with over 500 employees, could not but have a branch in Italy. The Center has a prestigious location in the heart of Rome, in Palazzo Santacroce, and the director is Oleg Osipov, a former journalist who worked as a correspondent in Italy for Moscow's Tass news agency. Apart from lunches and meetings with political representatives held directly at the residence of the Russian Ambassador Sergey Razov, the happenings at the more discreet location of Palazzo Santacroce allow us to see the more traditionally soft aspects of Russian power.

Although the director of the Center keeps a fairly low profile, his daughter Irina, on the other hand, has drawn attention on the Italian political scene. Born in 1988, Irina chairs another association that "supports" Moscow's cultural influence in Italy, the RIM, that aims to bring together young Italo-Russians. This young activist has a more explicit political role, participating in public debate in Italy through social networks, and now also appearing on national television shows such as *Nemo* on Rai 2 channel. Her point of view is simple: Putin is to be defended, as are his Italian allies, starting with the leader of the League (former Northern League) Matteo Salvini. Her polemics were already seen back in 2014, with the journalist Lucia Annunziata. The host of *In mezz'ora* on the Rai 3 channel had dared to criticize Matteo Salvini, suggesting that the numerous trips by League representatives to Moscow – the year was 2014 – could have been seen as betraying the West. God forbid. Irina Osipova objected, writing as follows:

> This journalist seems to me to be a lobotomized frog. That interview should be watched again in a couple of years, to recognize that Salvini is a bright mind

and has the balls to say certain things, especially regarding the subservience of European nations to the United States.³

Irina was not wrong. Not two, but four, years later, the "captain" of the League became Deputy Prime Minister, Interior Minister and the strong man of the coalition that began to lead the country after the elections of March 4, 2018.

The director of the Russian Center for Science and Culture in Rome and his daughter, president of the RIM, have drawn considerable attention, even ending up being accused by the Ukrainian television channel ICTV of being agents of the secret services of the Putin regime, operating to support Moscow's position in the war of information over the crisis with Kiev. According to the news report, Rossotrudnichestvo is the headquarters for propaganda operations in Italy. For her part, Irina Osipova stressed the lack of proof of connections with the Kremlin and the intelligence services, and at the same time claimed the merit of having supported initiatives in favor of the Donbas (the Ukrainian region involved in the military conflict between Moscow and Kiev). Here as well, there are numerous associations and committees that have sprouted like mushrooms – especially in the north of Italy – to collect funds and organize initiatives to foster support for Russia. The hat they wear is that of humanitarian assistance, but the relations between Italian politics, pro-Putin organizations and financial flows are certainly not trivial. Osipova, again, is one of the most active promoters of the *Sovranità* association, born in 2016 to support the candidacy of Matteo Salvini for the office of prime minister.

The galaxy of associations and entities that move with ease between Italy and Russia is truly vast, and it is almost impossible to determine precise borders. There are groups such as *Mille Patrie*, which in a certain sense culturally accompanied the shift of the League from a federalist force to a right-wing movement, or Campo Russo, a non-profit based in Naples run by Ekaterina Kornilkova (also indicated by Ukrainian TV as a Russian agent linked to the Embassy and Osipova's center). Naturally, we must not omit the value of more institutional organizations linked to economic interests, more than political ones, if it is actually possible to distinguish the two. On the web page of the Italian mission to Moscow we find the contact information for the Italy-Russia Chamber of Commerce (CCIR), whose president is Rosario Alessandrello, a manager who constructed his career at Tecnimont and was granted the Order of Friendship by President

Putin in person. Alessandrello also chairs the foundation named "Center for the Development of Italy–Russia Relations"; so his role goes beyond the CCIR.

The Chamber of Commerce is certainly an important instrument, as we can see by the quantity and quality of the Russians present in the organization, but also the presence as vice president of Luigi Pio Scordamaglia, who was once the president of the powerful food producers federation Federalimentare within Italy's largest industrial association, Confindustria. The industrial association can also count on Confindustria Russia, whose president is Ernesto Ferlenghi. Ferlenghi is a manager at Eni who is known publicly for having repeatedly intervened to take a position against the European sanctions imposed on Moscow, in newspapers such as *Messaggero* and *Libero*, and also Russian publications such as *Sputnik*. A conversation with him published in *Libero*, on April 1, 2018, was cited in a Tweet by Matteo Salvini, who made a solemn pledge: "When I'll be in government, the sanctions on Russia will go."[4] The elections had been held a little less than a month earlier, the League was considered one of the two winners, and Salvini was already proposing himself as the leader of the new majority. Who interviewed Ferlenghi? Gianluca Savoini, a journalist (he worked at the League's newspaper *la Padania* before becoming the director of the press office of the Lombardy Region when Roberto Maroni was president) but also the founder of *Lombardia Russia*, another crucial entity in the bilateral relations between the two countries, and above all the most important and celebrated bridge between the League headquarters and the Kremlin. We will speak more of this organization later when we look more directly at the relationship between Russia and Italian politics. Returning to the associations active on a business level, we should also mention GIM-Unimpresa, that brings together Italian businessmen in Russia, whose president is Giorgio Callegari of Assicurazioni Generali Russia. Among the partners we find another crucial player on the chessboard of Russian soft power in Italy: Conoscere Eurasia. The association was born in 2007, but in recent years it has become the preferred location for meetings with Russian interests in Italy. Here the key figure is Antonio Fallico, head of the Banca Intesa bank in Moscow, and undoubtedly the most influential Italian in Russia, including at the Kremlin. Conoscere Eurasia conducts activities that are not inferior to those of Rossotrudnichestvo, in terms of quantity and quality. The most important appointment is certainly the Verona Forum, a very important showcase for business and politics. To get an idea, even Pope Francis sent a message to the 2017 edition of the event.[5] It is sufficient to peruse the list of participants to see the strength of a relationship, between Italy and Russia, that is not limited to the energy business, however important: the dominant figure, including in relations with Rome, is Igor Sechin, the big boss of Rosneft who is at the top of the "Putin List" of figures sanctioned by the United States.

The places where Russian soft power is exercised in Italy are numerous, as we have seen. However, the network that has grown the most and manifested its weight, possibly even in electoral terms, is that pervading cybernetic space. There is where the power becomes sharper, and fearsome.

... to sharp power

Red Square has always exerted its charm on Italian media. In the postwar period the pro-Communist journalists and publications were the ones that looked kindly towards the Soviet regime. In the period of the Second Republic (starting in the 1990s), the good press continued above all thanks to the personal friendship between Putin and Silvio Berlusconi, who in addition to being prime minister several times, never stopped his activity as a publisher. The center-right newspapers and TV stations constantly showed a positive attitude towards Moscow. The flow of acritical information – a euphemism – not only was never interrupted, but actually increased starting at least in the early 2000s.

It was only with the explosion of the web and social networks, though, that Russia made the jump that currently worries the main Western intelligence agencies. The decision by the president of the Russian Federation and former KGB leader was incontrovertible: make massive and strategic investments in media. Russia Today was launched in 2005. The goal is not to speak of Russia but to talk about world events from Moscow's point of view. Thanks to the abundant funding that passes through the state Ria Novosti agency (formally the publisher), it took on the sexier name of RT and transformed into a made-in-Russia version of CNN. The channel broadcasts throughout the world and speaks multiple languages: from Arabic to English, Spanish to German and French. An all-news satellite channel is essential, but not sufficient. This is why the Kremlin decided to invest in a platform that truly has no borders, YouTube. In this global marketplace the channel has earned approximately 3 million followers and around 3 billion total views; numbers that turn heads. RT boasts that it was the first news channel to exceed 1 billion views on YouTube. Naturally the record didn't stop there, and continues to be driven, among other things, with the spread of conspiracy theories (which often cross over into the category of fake news, despite the abuse of the term).

RT does not use the Italian language but frequently has Italian guests. The engagement obtained by the Russian TV channel, and its social networks, is not trivial, and at the same time it is a litmus test allowing us to draw a map of the political forces most appreciated by Moscow. The interviews with Beppe Grillo and Matteo Salvini are often cited as an example of the relationship between the M5S, the League and Russia. The journalist Marcello Foa, designated by the Italian government as president of the state media company Rai, as a representative of the League, has been accused of being pro-Putin due to his collaboration with RT and *Sputnik*. As we saw in the previous chapters, the latter is the most serious Trojan horse used by the Russians to have a direct relationship with public opinion in the various countries, Italy included. *Sputnik*'s success is due to many factors, but certainly the method of refutation has a particular appeal for web users. In a nutshell, the aim is to instill doubts regarding the official stories proposed by traditional media (by now contemptuously defined as *mainstream*). With *Sputnik*, the conspiracy technique already seen in action on RT is presented with ever greater effect on the web.

(Successful) attempts at agenda setting

Sputnik's strategy is not only to win an increasing audience, but also to orient the agenda of public debate. In the United States there are now public CIA reports that openly describe the channel's influence, or better, the interference in various electoral processes carried out by the Kremlin's means of communication; the representatives of these publications are increasingly considered similar to "foreign agents." French President Emmanuel Macron rejected a request from the *Sputnik* correspondent to be accredited as a journalist at the Elysée Palace; a response to the incessant campaign carried out by the Russian site (in French) against his candidacy.

Unlike RT, *Sputnik* also has an Italian channel and is very active on the web and social networks. A Spanish company with expertise in big data analysis, named Alto Analytics, conducted a study in the period from February to July 2017.[6] Over 1 million posts and comments were monitored that had been generated by about 100,000 users who used the *Sputnik* site to then spread the virus of populist propaganda in particular feeding the fear of a migrant invasion. According to the data scientists at Alto Analytics, over 90 percent of the content that is used on social networks to circulate *Sputnik* (and RT) items channels an anti-immigration message. The messages are simple and revolve around the following arguments: the conviction that Italy is suffering from an "invasion" with negative economic and social consequences for Italians; criticism towards the way the Italian government and politicians have managed the immigration issue with an underlying anti-European message based on discrediting the EU or raising doubts about its role and the adaptation of Italy within the Union; the association of immigration with a lack of security, with crime and terrorism, and in some cases, with conspiracy theories claiming that the immigration crisis is part of a broader strategy to destabilize the country (the Soros argument).

As all digital communication experts explain, the difference is made not only by "direct" readers of a single publication online, but by the number of overall contacts that are generated by sharing on social networks and "bounces" on other blogs. This explains why the contents of RT on YouTube and *Sputnik* in all of its manifestations are able to have such a profound impact on national sentiment, including in Italy. In addition to the detailed numbers of the research conducted by the Spanish company, there are countless journalistic investigations that have identified a large network of sites and social network accounts that act as an echo chamber for Russian propaganda. Obviously, together with the messages that have a greater impact on each national debate, they also spread the fundamentals of Moscow's foreign policy. In Italy, the phenomenon is particularly widespread. The virtual network is naturally even more extensive than the traditional territorial network made up of a myriad of associations and institutions that even at the local level, deal with the issue of Eurasian cooperation (translated: shifting Italian interests towards those of the Kremlin). It is truly a difficult task to identify all of the pro-Russia sites active in Italy and involved in propaganda on domestic issues as well.

Looking specifically at the Russian experience of *Sputnik* as a model of communication, in 2014 League secretary Matteo Salvini stopped the daily publication of *la Padania* and in 2016 inaugurated an online portal whose masthead is very transparently consistent with its program: *Il Populista*. The leader himself, in announcing the birth of the portal, described it as a "voice that is audacious, instinctive, out-of-control ... and a little bit pissed off."[7] Here as well the scheme is the same as we have seen previously. Conspiracy theories with a massive dose of facts told through the lens of post-truth. In practice, the border between information, propaganda and fake news is increasingly thin.[8] There are three other sites often reported for fake news, whether published directly or picked up from others, that act similarly. These are *TzeTze*, *La Fucina* and *La Cosa*, whose domains are part of the Milanese network headed by Davide Casaleggio, the tutelary deity of the Rousseau association, and through this, of the Five-Star Movement. *Infoa5Stelle* is another web address, accompanied by a very well-read Facebook page, created and managed by Marco Mignogna, a M5S activist, who is also the owner of a *cult* domain in the political galaxy close to the Kremlin: IostoconPutin.info ("I stand with Putin," a domain currently for sale). Then there are portals such as *Catena Umana* that is controlled by the entrepreneur Vincenzo Todaro, who by himself manages about 20 sites with ambiguous titles such as skytg24news, tgcom24news and repubblica24.com, that essentially attempt to hijack readers using the names of real news channels. An investigation by the American site *Buzzfeed* also reported on the information manipulation activities (in the opinion of the authors of the report, given great emphasis by the *New York Times*) by two enormously popular sites on the web and on Facebook: *Direttanews24* and *iNews24*, both owned by the entrepreneur from Frascati Giancarlo Colono. With his agency Web365, Colono has registered almost two hundred domains. As can be expected, the agenda is the same.[9] It fits well with strongly anti-immigration sites such as *ImolaOggi* or those oriented towards a more general debate such as *L'Intellettuale Dissidente*, *Il Talebano*, *L'Antidiplomatico*, *Il Fattaccio*, *Voci dalla Strada*, *Opinione-Pubblica* and many others. Another case that has drawn considerable attention, including on the other side of the Atlantic, is that of *Byoblu*, the video blog of Claudio Messora, one of the original Five-Star gurus (considered by some to be one of the movement's ideologues) and formerly a consultant for the movement at the Senate. He has been suspected of direct links with Russian disinformation, which he denies, however. With the accusation of spreading fake news, he was suspended from AdSense, the Google advertising platform. Even Italian Head of State Sergio Mattarella got involved in the polemics triggered by this blog founded in 2007. Naturally, among many more or less impromptu newcomers, we cannot forget those who were pillars of pro-Soviet information in the past, and are pro-Putin now. Giulietto Chiesa remains very strong on the web, social networks and also traditional media. He is also regularly present on *Sputnik* and has his own publishing initiative, *Pandora.tv*.

The list could go on for many pages, but by now the reader should have an idea of the nature of the very powerful propaganda machine able to produce a large echo effect, and at least in the cited cases, one with a sufficiently clear foreign policy orientation. It could be objected that these are the actions of isolated individuals, not linked with each other except by a common sentiment. Even if this were true, it would not take anything away from the Russian Bear's seductive power that is much less soft than at the time of print media or generalist TV. In reality, in addition to the political connections that we will try to present later, we must also cite the economic links between many of the subjects in question, that are a part of the Italian galaxy of pro-Russian information, whose methods and aims they share.

Who funds online propaganda?

An initial cutaway of the economic connections among many of these sites came to light with the investigation we have already cited that was conducted by *BuzzFeed* and circulated by the *New York Times* in November 2017, regarding the mother of all defeats for the former Italian Prime Minister and Democratic Party Secretary Matteo Renzi: the constitutional referendum of December 4, 2016. At the time, Renzi, the former mayor of Florence, had reported the threat of Russian interference, as confirmed by the alarm launched in Washington. The *BuzzFeed* investigation came a year later[10]. It consisted of an 11-page report to stress all of the connections between the sites of the Five-Star area and the contents of Russian propaganda spread through the *Sputnik* and RT circuit. There was a detail that to that point had remained unknown: all of these domains (from *IostoconPutin.info* to *TzeTze*) collected financial resources with the same identification code assigned by Google Analytics (a service which records visits to various sites), the same AdSense number (through which the giant of Mountain View manages and remunerates advertisements) and even the same template on the contact page. Since most of these sites were linked to the Five-Star Movement, the movement's members had specified that these were independent, non-official initiatives, and that the convergence was the result of the actions of an activist. After the publication of the article in the *New York Times*, which was then picked up in the Italian media, the blog of Beppe Grillo – founder of the M5S – reduced, but did not entirely interrupt, the links to these sites.

The most intriguing, and in a certain sense surprising, piece of news, however, was that the web site *Noi con Salvini* (the parallel movement to the League calling for the "captain" to become prime minister) had the same IP address. A few days after the *BuzzFeed* investigation was published, the League's director of digital communications, Luca Morisi, had to admit that indeed their site shared the Google codes with sites outside of their political movement. More specifically, Morisi's argument, as cited by the New York newspaper, was that the site *Noi con Salvini* had also been built by a former Five-Star supporter, pasting the codes of his page in support of M5S onto the page of the pro-Salvini site (in addition to the pages of pro-Russian conspiracy sites such as IostoconPutin.info). The leaders of the two parties immediately denied any connections with Moscow and promised to change the codes. Google's policies do not allow for penetrating the wall of privacy around the registered user of the IP code to which all of the advertising money flowed for months. Given the extent of the audience reached by the totality of the domains involved, we are not speaking of negligible amounts. Another doubt which remains, regards the method by which these proceeds were divided between the different sites. The suspicion of a stronger mixture between the Grillo and Salvini supporters in the name of Putin – made explicit in the *New York Times* article – was soon dismissed as fanciful or the result of a maneuver by Renzi to justify the imminent defeat. The doubts regarding the conspiracy prevailed, and this "coincidence" was soon dismissed, although it reemerged sporadically in subsequent months. Ultimately Di Maio and Salvini actually signed the government pact, that among other things included an official opening to Putin (with a contractual commitment to review the mechanism of the sanctions against Russia) as a key and central point of their agreement. There are no elements that can prove a cause- effect connection between these coincidences, but what cannot be denied is that the web, through effective manipulation, was if not a catalyst, at least a precursor to the political scenario that then came about in Italy.

Before going into the details of the relations between Moscow and Italy political forces, we will consider a few more points on the ability of the pro-Russian communication network to obtain funding. The newspaper *la Repubblica* assigned the journalists Carlo Bonini and Giuliano Foschini to conduct an investigation that was published the day before the referendum, on December 3, 2016; this investigation was also overwhelmed by the events after the vote.[11] Their analysis started from the assumption that fake news and conspiracy sites in general benefit from a particular level of curiosity among people on the web. This automatically translates into visitor traffic and publicity, and thus money. Through the testimony of a repented "faker," the Italian journalists reconstructed the way in which in social media it can be relatively easy to multiply the number of visitors and make false or even only plausible content go viral; obtaining a profit that, in turn, goes through the intermediaries, the advertising brokers. The companies that worked with these sites, *Repubblica* explained, have names such as Criteo, Chamaleon and Adnow. Lastly, one particular company was noted ("a startup that shines for its aggressiveness and profitability"): Clickio. If we look carefully, it seems to be a satellite of AdLabs, one of the most important advertising concessionaires in Russia. The suspicion – immediately denied by the interested parties – is that the much higher remuneration offered by Clickio is conditional upon the fact that the publishers/clients share their pro-Russian positions on their sites. In this case as well, following the advertising trail, we end up at online newspapers such as *Direttanews* or *L'Antidiplomatico*. It seems to be the closing of the circle, at least in the journalistic investigation.

In this intricate kaleidoscope of political, economic and cultural interests, there are no apparent crimes and we cannot reach the conclusion that the conspirators have hatched a perfect plot to defeat an Atlanticist majority. A measured assessment is necessary to understand the dimensions of a phenomenon that perhaps by itself is not decisive for electoral results, but is also not indifferent in the construction of perceptions in public opinion. From Moscow's standpoint, it can be considered a success that goes beyond the dimension of soft power. It is decidedly sharp.

From the web to the polls

Italy's foreign policy is based on some pillars that have never been called into question by the numerous governments that have occupied Palazzo Chigi since the end of Fascism. These are: Europe's link with the United States, and thus with NATO, the attention towards the Mediterranean, and lastly, friendship with Russia (previously the Soviet Union).

To describe the positive attitude towards Moscow as something new introduced by the M5S–League government would definitely be an exaggeration. In a country like Italy, that during the Cold War was on the border of the Iron Curtain between the two dominant blocs, the choice of the Atlantic Alliance was never questioned, but neither was the preferential relationship with the East. The leadership of the Christian Democratic Party, to the shock of US administrations, never decided to outlaw the Italian Communist Party (the largest in the West) or to prevent it from being financed in rubles. The unifying view of Italy that prevailed in the post-war period and the subsequent link between Rome and Moscow was never broken. To the contrary, from Giulio Andreotti to Bettino Craxi, from Silvio Berlusconi to Romano Prodi and Matteo Renzi, whoever had government responsibility realistically managed this particular relationship. With the meeting between Vladimir Putin and George Bush at Pratica di Mare in 2002, Italy's presumed role as a bridge between Washington and Moscow was extolled, perhaps beyond its objective merits. In reality, at the time Silvio Berlusconi was particularly appreciated by both leaders, but outside of our borders, such a large ambition is difficult for Rome to sustain. Yet this is one of the greatest and most shared aspirations of our foreign policy. On the other hand, while the personal relations between Berlusconi and Putin are well known, another relationship is just as important, and has passed the test of time: Russia's links with Romano Prodi from the time he was president of the European Commission.

In his brief interlude at Palazzo Chigi (the seat of the Italian government), Enrico Letta, another figure respected by the European elites, also chose a line of continuity towards Moscow. He was the only head of a large European government who was present at the opening of the Sochi Olympic Games in February 2014, when Barack Obama, Angela Merkel, François Hollande and David Cameron intentionally stayed away. As we have already written, like other large sports events, the Olympics are an event with considerable political implications, and the Italian presence was widely noted. Matteo Renzi, who took over the Italian government a few days later in that same February 2014, also had to deal with the crisis in Ukraine. The neo-prime minister's initial reaction was not a decisive condemnation of the Russian invasion and support for sanctions against Moscow. After a little more than two years, in October 2016, it was again the Italian head of government who at the European Council opposed sanctions against Russia for the bombing of Aleppo, thus blocking the proposal by France, Germany and the United Kingdom: "Russia is our largest neighbor, the one most closely linked to the Syrian question," "Europe and Russia must keep a channel of dialogue and communication open," and "Sanctions are not a deterrent."[12] These are the words used by Matteo Renzi at the end of the Brussels summit. When Paolo Gentiloni arrived at Palazzo Chigi, the terms of the relationship with Moscow did not change. During the course of his term as prime minister, Italy had to manage the Skripal case, the poisoning of the former Russian spy in London which according to the UK government was the result of a mission ordered by the Kremlin. This case provoked a very harsh reaction against the Putin regime. The United States and Europe immediately took strong positions, with no hesitation. Italy remained a step behind, or even more than one. "Condemnation does not automatically lead to escalation and does not close the necessary room for dialogue with Russia," was the much softer declaration that came from Prime Minister Gentiloni.[13] Does the fact that the M5S–League government led by Giuseppe Conte is based on a contract which openly and clearly expresses a pro-Russian position (including on sanctions related to Ukraine) thus represent continuity or discontinuity with the Italian position of "we are with Washington but also with Moscow"? This is not the place for such an assessment. What interests us here is to investigate, on a cultural level, the case of Russian influence, whether soft or sharp, with respect to Italian internal politics. From this standpoint, the political events of recent years can be read from an angle that does indeed show innovative, non-negligible aspects.

Linked, from the start

The most interesting case is certainly that of the League. Salvini's relationship with the leadership of the Putin regime is closely tied to the political rise of the then-young leader of the party. In 2013 the movement founded by Umberto Bossi was in full crisis, as scandals had overwhelmed the political group that had made federalism its rallying cry. Not even the secretaryship of Roberto Maroni had succeeded in stopping the hemorrhage of votes. The party was considered finished, and it was in this climate that the leadership decided to entrust operations to a young northerner who was particularly active, especially in communications. Matteo Salvini became the federal secretary of the Northern League on December 15, 2013 at the Turin Congress. At the *Lingotto* conference center were representatives of the most anti-EU right-wing groupings from around Europe, and also a delegation from United Russia, Putin's party-state, with the parliamentarians Viktor Komov and Alexej Komov. The confrontation between the Kremlin and the new Ukrainian government had already begun, due to Kiev's desire to join the EU. Salvini had already taken a position in favor of Moscow. An alliance was born that grew considerably with the Kiev crisis. It was precisely at the end of 2013 that *Lombardia Russia* was founded, the association run by Savoini already cited above. In the same period Putin launched the new strategy of influence through the media (with the cited cases of RT and *Sputnik*), but also intensifying relations with political movements and single European leaders, especially those based at the Parliament in Brussels. It was November 29, 2014 when the journalist Leonardo Coen wrote in the newspaper *Il Fatto Quotidiano*:

> The League could become the effective key to Italy. As for money he added – the indirect channels to help friends are many, and the Russians are masters at this: they operate through numerous companies in Serbia, Hungary, Cyprus, Finland, Spain, Switzerland, France and England.[14]

Apart from the unproven references to potential funding of pro-Russian political movements, what stands out, less than a year after the coronation of Salvini, is that there were already such explicit views of the link with Moscow. In reality, there is nothing to be surprised about. The leader of the League immediately embarked on trips to Russia, and ultimately ended up getting his meeting with Putin, although on the margins of an international summit in Milan. It was October 17, 2004, and Salvini was accompanied by Savoini and Claudio d'Amico, another key figure in the relations between the League and the Kremlin. He told the party newspaper, *la Padania*: "It was an exciting and cordial meeting. Putin called the League a serious and courageous movement. And he praised

Lombardy and Veneto's work to overcome the embargo." In a short space of time the League established itself, transparently, as a political force whose priorities include a special relationship with the regime of Czar Vladimir. The flights to and from Moscow became more frequent. Alexander Dugin, considered the ideologue of the Russian leader, also came to Italy, and defined the League as "the last hope for Italy," also explaining the meaning of the alliance with groupings such as that of Le Pen in France.

We now go to June 2015. The meetings, initiatives, interviews and contacts multiply, as does the attention of Italian and foreign media. This is no way slows down the plot. Rather, on March 6, 2017 something happened which in a certain sense was extraordinary. In Russia an official agreement was signed between the League and United Russia, Vladimir Putin's party that has been in power since the end of the nineties. The parties to the agreement are, respectively, Matteo Salvini and the Russian parliamentarian Sergey Zheleznyak, who agree on information exchange between the two political parties, among other things. The text states as follows:

> The Parties will consult each other and exchange information on current events in the Russian Federation and the Republic of Italy, on bilateral and international relations, on the exchange of experience in the sphere of the party structure, organized labor, policies for youth, economic development, and in other fields of mutual interest.[15]

A year later, in March 2018, Salvini would find himself considered to be one of the two winners of the general elections, and despite some internal and external difficulties, he would make it into government. The worries of Western allies were on par with the enthusiasm from Russia. The parliamentary representatives of German intelligence went as far as questioning the collaborative relationship with the Italian secret services due to the affinity with the Russian regime. Was this an exaggeration, or merely a signal? The fact is that the existence of a public protocol of collaboration between Salvini and the leaders of United Russia is simultaneously both a masterpiece for the Kremlin and a crushing defeat for Western allies. On the other hand, the League leader can certainly not be accused of being a double-dealer. His positions have always been very explicit. As deputy prime minister and Interior Minister he flew to Moscow for the final game of the soccer World Cup (speaking of the value of sports events) and there he met with his Interior counterpart and the leaders of the National Security Council, who by the way are all top figures in the ranks of former KGB agents. At these meetings, as he himself announced on social networks, Savoini, the president of *Lombardia Russia* and Salvini's ambassador to the Kremlin, was also present. To *Il Foglio*, that had reported on the institutional anomaly of the presence of a third party at meetings where sensitive issues for international security were presumably discussed, it was stated that no matters covered by any type of secrecy were touched on.[16] So everything was said to be fine. Just as the fact that a long, private conversation took place between the new deputy prime minister and the Russian ambassador Razov took place a few days after the swearing in and on the margins of a reception organized at Villa Abamelek to celebrate Russian independence was considered routine. In this case as well, Salvini had the merit of not playing coy, but affirming that he has "clear ideas" on the question of sanctions, and that the government will discuss the issue in Brussels.

The overlapping between an institutional role (the Interior Ministry manages a large quantity of delicate and sensitive information) and a position of political leadership can create some incidents. At the beginning, a selfie was shared on social media showing classified documents, that fortunately were not legible; then, public safety documents were again published on personal channels. There were many other cases of "mixing" that were much more visible than cases involving previous political ministers, including due to Salvini's abundant use of the web. One particularly important episode that was not much reported on in the media regards a Tweet the Interior Minister sent on the evening of August 10, 2018, when he retweeted and commented on a fake story regarding a group of immigrants who were said to have launched a protest to request the possibility to see the satellite television channels operated by Sky.[17] The item was a total invention spread by the site *VoxNews* and picked up by other online publications, until it was found to be pure disinformation without any basis, as declared by the local Prefecture well before Salvini's Tweet. The fact that a minister of the Republic amplifies a piece of fake news is not very flattering, but the fact that he did it after the news had already been denied by local offices under his own ministry has a certain effect. The media placed more attention on a different event: the publication by the celebrated American journalist Lally Weymouth of an interview with the leader of the League in the *Washington Post* on July 19, 2018.[18] Readers around the world discovered that the authoritative representative of the Italian government's position on the annexation of Crimea by Russia is that it was legitimate, due to the popular referendum.

This is not a new position, but many foreign observers were surprised by the fact that once Salvini made it to a position of government responsibility, his pro-Russian position did not change one bit, a position that is so strong that he did not even cite the Minsk agreements. The Tweets, the interviews, and the contract establishing the government program, clearly indicate the international positioning of the head of the League. Although Prime Minister Conte did not veto the renewal of the EU sanctions on Russia, and although Foreign Minister Moavero explained in Parliament that the Italian government's position on Crimea is that stated in official statements in international venues (essentially contradicting Salvini and his interview with the *Washington Post*), under the current government Italy finds itself in a new position in the heart of Europe, moving the balance much more to the east than to the west.

Indeed, relations with Moscow are not managed only by the League, but also by the other government partner, the Five-Star Movement. The links between M5S and Russia are not limited to the (very considerable) space of the infosphere. There have been numerous trips to Moscow and visits to Ambassador Razov in recent years. The spokesmen for this line of dialogue are principally Alessandro Di Battista, a reserve leader of the movement, Manlio Di Stefano, who became Undersecretary of Foreign Affairs, and Vito Petrocelli, promoted to Chairman of the Senate Foreign Affairs Committee. In their case as well, their political activity is perfectly legitimate and carried out in the light of day, just as the public positions they stake out on international affairs overlap entirely with those of Russia, and not only on the question of Ukraine. If a web has been woven by the Kremlin around Italy, there can be no doubt: the threads are strong and durable.

If the trolls enter the action

To this point we have analyzed Russian influence in Italy through organizations active there, through the vast network operating on the web and social networks, and lastly thanks to the direct relationship with political forces. This influence does not necessarily mean interference. However in both Italy and the United States the intelligence services and judicial institutions are beginning to take very seriously the possibility that a little hand (or a large hand) from Russia is acting to manipulate democratic processes and free information in the West. Sitting in the dock is the IRA, the Internet Research Agency we have already cited, according to the formal and well-documented accusations brought by former FBI Director Robert Mueller in the Russiagate investigation. As we have seen in the previous chapters, this is an agency based in Saint Petersburg known for being a "troll factory" par excellence. Founded in 2013 (a crucial year, we repeat) and considered an operational arm of the Kremlin, it is credited with being the central junction for the most important disinformation activities, including in Italy. Before trying to figure out what may have really happened here, we will attempt to explain what we mean when speaking of trolls. The context is that of social media, where – at least until now – the big players such as Facebook and Twitter allow for the opening of accounts that do not correspond to actual physical people. These profiles acquire importance the larger the number of their followers or friends are. Many precise techniques exist to create active subjects on social networks that have the goal of transmitting particular contents or buzzwords. We could say that the goal is to spread the virus and infect public debate. There are many profiles (and also blogs) managed by flesh and blood people who do the work as a profession (up to even more than 100 each), while others are bots, meaning robots that automatically share specific social messages. They do it immediately, without the need for a click by a human operator. The sum of these tools, together with the possibility to profile entire communities of online users, has made it possible to spread buzzwords, fears, anxiety and expectations that otherwise would have had a much lower weight in public opinion, thus having an impact on public preferences and the voting intentions of citizens. When conducted by foreign states with malicious intent (such as in the case of Russia), this activity represents a concrete threat to democracy and thus to national security. Number 55 Savushkina Street in Saint Petersburg, the offices of the IRA, appears to be the operational epicenter of this tsunami of disinformation that is shaking the United States and Europe (without counting the operations conducted by the Russian secret services, the FSB and the GRU, the subject of a specific report issued by US intelligence on January 6, 2017).

The fact that Italy may have been a victim of this manipulation is now the subject of (at least) one investigation by the Public Prosecutor's Office of Rome. This is in part based on the accusations, echoed in Washington, of a specific web and social campaign against the president of the republic at the end of 2018, who was guilty of blocking the creation of the Conte government by vetoing the designation of Paolo Savona as Economics Minister. If the courts, in Italy and the United States or elsewhere, were to find specific evidence of actions by foreign subjects, an unprecedented scenario would arise, with unpredictable consequences. In the meantime, not being able to rely on truths demonstrated legally, we will try to rewind the tape with the public information available. The European Popular Party, for example, has written a document entitled *Russia's Disinformation Undermining Western Democracy*.[19] In the approved resolution we find a very detailed accusation:

> EU Member States are facing an unprecedented threat to their democratic societies. Russian propaganda, disinformation campaigns and continuous support for anti-European political forces are undermining the European project, transatlantic cooperation and Western democracies in general … This crisis has in fact reached an alarming level.

That was in March 2017, four years after the founding of the IRA and almost two years after the article "The Agency" in which Adrian Chen first informed public opinion of the existence of this troll factory in the pages of the *New York Times*.[20]

Let us return to Italy in the spring of 2017, less than one year before the elections there. Barack Obama, no longer president of the United States, was in Milan to participate in a conference on sustainability, and met with Renzi (who was also no longer in office by then). According to journalistic accounts that were not denied, in talking to the secretary of the PD Obama stressed the worries about Russian interference in Italy, including in view of the elections. This was certainly not the first alert originating in America. The correspondent of the newspaper *La Stampa*, Paolo Mastrolilli, reported on a very detailed US intelligence report on Moscow's offensive to influence policy in Rome, which was not denied.[21] The facts refer to the fall of 2016. According to the journalist, the emissaries from Washington had identified the potential terminals ("points of contact") of this operation as the Five-Star Movement and the League. According to Mastrolilli, the US Embassy did not believe it could take a public position on the issue "in order not to jeopardize the possibility to work with all Italian political forces." However, he wrote, "the alarm had become systemic."

In December 2017 another alarming report arrived. The former Vice President of the United States Joe Biden wrote a piece together with the former Undersecretary of Defense Michael Carpenter in the famous magazine *Foreign Affairs*.[22] The essay, entitled "How to stand up to the Kremlin," is based on the conviction that Putin has launched a domestic and international campaign to preserve power, based on corruption and military and political interference. This strategy is claimed to pass through the destabilization of Western democracies. In this context, Biden and Carpenter cite the Russian influence on the Italian constitutional referendum of December 4, 2016 and add that "A similar Russian effort is now under way to support the nationalist Northern League and the populist Five Star Movement in Italy's upcoming parliamentary elections." Naturally, the authors mention precisely the IRA as an instrument used to spread fake news and manipulate information. In a subsequent interview with *La Stampa*, Carpenter explained that,

> Russian disinformation operations are those of the Saint Petersburg IRA because some deserters have explained exactly how it operates. There are many other Russian networks for trolls and we would be naïve to believe that all of the activity is limited to the IRA. This institution represents a good parameter, together with RT and *Sputnik*, to understand the type of messages the Kremlin wishes to spread.[23]

The former Pentagon official from the Obama Administration carefully highlights all of the links between Moscow and Italy, but specifies:

> I have no proof of Russian financing of Italian political parties, but I encourage you to investigate and follow the money, because it is very likely to be happening. There are various vehicles, explains Carpenter. In general the Kremlin does not employ direct agents of the state, such as diplomats. They do it with oligarchs, companies linked to Russia, or other proxies that are hard to identify. The money then goes to shell companies and is very hard to discover.[24]

Thus there is no proof, but once again, an authoritative voice indicates a precise danger (which by the way is always denied by the relevant parties in Italy, such as the League).

December 9, 2017. A few days later the former Secretary General of NATO, Rasmussen, would repeat the alarm ("Putin does not want to make Italy great, but to use it").[25] A few hours earlier the Vice President of United Russia, Sergey Zheleznyak, had denied funding Italian parties, but spoke of "exchange of experiences" and cited relations with the Five-Star Movement. In the meantime, the warning by Biden and Carpenter came to the attention of the Copasir (the Italian parliamentary commission that deals with intelligence), where the directors of the two intelligence services, Alberto Manenti and Mario Parenti, were called to testify. The heads of the internal and external agencies confirmed the constant monitoring of the possible foreign incursions during the election campaign, but also admitted they had not gathered sufficient evidence in relation to presumed Russian interference in the constitutional referendum of December 2016.

After Biden's accusation was dismissed, another came, again from a Democrat in the US Senator Ben Cardin delivered a document to Congress and the public of over 200 pages dedicated precisely to Russian interference in the West.[26] The case of Italy is dealt with in three pages, using open sources and again raising the suspicion of funding of the Northern League by the Kremlin's security services. Nothing particularly new, except that it quotes a declaration by the US Ambassador to Rome, Lewis Eisenberg. The Republican representative sent to Italy by Donald Trump states that he shares the "worries regarding Russian aggression in Europe, including disinformation campaigns and malicious activities of influence." This position is made public in January 2018. A few weeks go by, and on February 17 Paolo Mastrolilli returns in the pages of *La Stampa* with an investigation telling of five Twitter accounts, that had been dormant until 2015, that published 160,000 Tweets with favorable messages towards the Kremlin, the League and the Five-Star Movement.[27] The article clearly describes the mechanism that allows for multiplying the interactions of these likely fake accounts. Despite the effort expended in the investigation, the Italian newspaper is unable to break through all of the barriers set up to protect the real identity of the owners of these profiles. The techniques used, however, mirror those of the Russian troll factories such as the IRA. Is this a coincidence? Mastrolilli cannot give a definitive response but finds it useful to note the case. A few days later – again in February 2018 – the Special Prosecutor Mueller publishes information (a 37-page report) that is said to confirm the involvement of the Saint Petersburg agency in actions to interfere in Italy. The report cites various accounts that are claimed to have operated from Russia in English and Italian.[28] The focus of the investigation is Russiagate in the US, but the trails that lead to Italy emerge clearly. As the March 4 vote approached, just 24 hours in advance Italian intelligence announced a special effort to thwart the threat of a hacker attack (that evidently was considered to be concrete). So the secret services were preparing for a digital war, although they reassured everyone that there was nothing illegal about the accounts reported by *La Stampa* – even though two of them were independently suspended by the American provider after the publication of the journalistic investigation.

Additional accusations regarding the activity of the IRA in Italy would come only at the beginning of August 2018. Two experts from Clemson University, Darren Linvill and Patrick Warren, conducted an investigation published on the web site *FiveThirtyEight* run by Nate Silver.[29] An analysis of approximately 3 million Tweets sent starting on June 19, 2015 from an unspecified number of accounts – which however Twitter had already recognized as being linked to the Internet Research Agency of Saint Petersburg – found that at least eight "Italian" accounts and 12,610 Tweets had been created in Italy through a VPN, which as we have seen allows to conceal the actual location from which the digital content is generated. These accounts did not spread particularly evident disinformation (Twitter blocked them as soon as the link with Russia was discovered), but they confirmed the threat of the Kremlin's trolls on the Italian web. Talk of interference in Italy's elections also came from Facebook's head of security, Alex Stamos.[30] The director of Italian intelligence, Alessandro Pansa, was more cautious: he stressed to the Copasir that there is not sufficient evidence to report foreign aggression in Italy through cyberspace.[31]

If on the one hand this position is reassuring, on the other it takes nothing away from the Kremlin's ability to influence the public space, regardless of any interference that has or has not been established yet. It has been explained clearly by the director of the Forensic Research Lab of Washington, Graham Brookie. Upon arriving in Italy on the eve of the March 4 vote, in an interview with *Formiche.net* he said:

> In our daily activities we note that in Italy as well there is widespread fake news on issues such as immigration and economics, for example. The level of alert we see is also undoubtedly high. However – he stresses – there are no

elements that prove the existence of an organized disinformation campaign in your country like that we have seen in other nations, where there have been important leaks.³²

The American expert, who has worked at the White House's National Security Council in the past, explained the situation as follows:

> The reason is fairly obvious, and has to do principally with the fact that until now the Kremlin, the largest producer of fake news to influence elections with tools such as the state media *Sputnik*, bots and trolls, has not had much of a need to force Italian parties to be pro-Russian. Due to tradition, proximity, political and economic choices, or also true friendship between leaders, Italy already maintains positions close to those of Moscow. This means the country doesn't need to receive particular attention.

We see the strength of soft power that becomes sharp, without a great deal of effort.

Notes

[1] P. Kreko, *The Russian Connection: The Spread of Pro-Russian Policies on the European Far Right*, Political Capital, 2014.

[2] M.H. Van Herpen, *Putin's Propaganda Machine: Soft Power and Russian Foreign Policy*, Lanham–London, Rowman & Littlefield, 2016.

[3] G. Ponziano, "Salvini si è fatto scudo per Putin," *Italia Oggi*, 11/12/2014, www.italiaoggi.it.

[4] "Forza Salvini, elimina le sanzioni contro Mosca. Intervista di Gianluca Savoini a Ernesto Ferlenghi," *Libero*, 1/4/2018.

[5] "Saluto del Papa a Forum eurasiatico Verona: 'Curare casa comune,' "*Askanews*, 19/10/2017, www.askanews.it.

[6] Alto Data Analytics, *The Construction of Anti-Immigration Electoral Messages in Italy: The Role of Foreign Media in the Anti-Immigration Debate One Year Before the 2018 Election*, 2018.

[7] In August 2018 Salvini's post was still accessible at the address: https://www.facebook.com/salviniofficial/posts/benvenuto-a-il-populista-voce-audace-istintiva-fuori-controllo-e-un-po-incazzata/10153752272728155/.

[8] L. Bianchi, "Abbiamo chiesto a un esperto di bufale di analizzare il nuovo sito di Matteo Salvini," *Vice*, 12/5/2016, www.vice.com.

[9] A. Nardelli, C. Silverman, "One of the biggest alternative media networks in Italy is spreading anti-immigrant news and misinformation on Facebook," *Buzzfeed News*, 21/11/2017, www.buzzfeed.com; J. Horowitz, "Italy, bracing for electoral season of fake news, demands Facebook's help," *New York Times*, 24/11/2017, www.nytimes.com.

[10] *Ibid.*

[11] C. Bonini, G. Foschini, "Così si finanzia la fabbrica delle fake news," *la Repubblica*, 3/12/2016.

[12] I. Caizzi, "Siria, il summit notturno e le sanzioni alla Russia: alla fine vince il no di Renzi," *Corriere della Sera*, 21/10/2016, www.corriere.it.

[13] "Caso Skripal, Consiglio europeo condanna Mosca. Gentiloni: 'Conclusioni condivise, ma non chiudiamo il dialogo,'" *Il Fatto Quotidiano*, 23/3/2018, www.ilfattoquotidiano.it.

[14] L. Coen, "Lega, crescono i rapporti con il Cremlino. Salvini: se arrivassero i soldi li accetterei," *Il Fatto Quotidiano*, 29/11/2014, www.ilfattoquotidiano.it.

[15] The full text of the agreement is included in the book: F. Sapettini, A. Tabacchini, *Da Pontida a Mosca: Gli accordi fra Putin e la Lega Nord*, Edizioni Samovar, 2018.

[16] D. Allegranti, "Che ci faceva il putiniano Gianluca Savoini con Salvini in Russia," *Il Foglio*, 18/7/2018, www.ilfoglio.it.

[17] "Salvini e la bufala dei migranti che pretendono l'abbonamento a Sky," *la Repubblica*, 10/8/2018, www.repubblica.it.

[18] L. Weymouth, "Italy has done a lot – maybe too much," *The Washington Post*, 19/7/2018, www.washingtonpost.com.

[19] European People's Party, *Russian Disinformation Under in western Democracy*, Resolution adopted by EPP Congress, St. Julian's (Malta), March 29–30, 2017, http://www.epp.eu.

[20] A. Chen, "The agency," *New York Times*, 6/6/2015.

[21] P. Mastrolilli, "Offensiva russa in Italia, le prove consegnate a Roma dal Dipartimento di Stato," *La Stampa*, 27/11/2017, www.lastampa.it.

[22] J.R. Biden Jr, M. Carpenter, "How to stand up to the Kremlin," *Foreign Affairs*, January/February 2018, www.foreignaffairs.com.

[23] P. Mastrolilli, "Troll, bot e associazioni culturali. Così la Russia ha sabotato il referendum in Italia," interview with Michael Carpenter, *La Stampa*, 9/12/2017, www.lastampa.it.

[24] A shell company is a business that is used to hide the (often illegal) activities of another person or business (such as money laundering).

[25] P. Mastrolilli, "Rasmussen: Putin vuole utilizzare l'Italia per dividere l'Unione e abbattere le sanzioni," interview with Fogh Rasmussen, *La Stampa*, 14/12/2017, www.lastampa.it.

[26] US Senate Committee on Foreign Relations, "US Senator Ben Cardin releases report detailing two decades of Putin's attacks on democracy, calling for policy changes to counter Kremlin threat ahead of 2018, 2020 election," 10/1/2018, www.foreign.senate.gov.

[27] P. Mastrolilli, "Elezioni, dal web attacchi filorussi," *La Stampa*, 17/2/2018.

[28] *United States of America v. Internet Research Agency, Criminal No. (18 USC. §§ 2, 371, 1349, 1028A)*, Case 1:18-cr-00032-DLF, February 2018, www.justice.gov.

[29] O. Roeder, "Why we're sharing 3 million Russian troll tweets," *FiveThirtyEight*, 31/7/2018, fivethirtyeight.com.

[30] P. Mastrolilli, "Fake news, si apre il fronte di Facebook. Interferenze russe sul voto del 4 marzo," *La Stampa*, 5/8/2018, www.lastampa.it.

[31] "'Attacchi troll' a Mattarella, pm Roma indagano per attentato alla libertà del presidente: 'Account creato su snodo Milano,'" *Il Fatto Quotidiano*, 6/8/2018, www.ilfattoquotidiano.it.

[32] M. Pierri, "Perché in Italia la disinformazione russa è meno aggressiva. L'analisi del DFRLab (Atlantic Council)," *Formiche.net*, 1/3/2018, www.formiche.net.

6   China is Close, Very Close

Unlike Russian trolls, who entered the public consciousness in a major way (or at least into the more attentive part of it), the Chinese influence in Italy is an argument that, if it isn't taboo, is certainly a phantom. Relations with Beijing are spoken of principally in economic terms, and in a positive manner. The Italian governments, from Renzi to that led by Giuseppe Conte, look for the possibility to attract new investments. A fine idea, of course. The only limit is that of not considering the other side of the coin: the effects of Chinese penetration in strategic sectors of the country and the possible consequences on national security. If the Kremlin also acts on a political level with a certain energy, Mao's grandchildren have a different attitudes which was clearly summarized by Henry Kissinger, who in his book *China* explained the preference for tortuosity rather than clashes:[1] achieving results with patience and gradualism, like in *weiki*, a table game with 180 pieces per side in which various goals are pursued simultaneously. Unlike the Western game of chess, no checkmate is necessary here. The result is obtained with the logic of a minimal advantage, that which a non-expert, non-Chinese eye may not even recognize. This is the meaning of an invasion which is soft, and at times sharp; an approach that concerns Italy as well, considerably.

The Dragon and the Boot

Italy is the number three destination in Europe for Chinese investments, as stated by Angelino Alfano when in 2017 he held the position of Minister of Foreign Affairs and International Cooperation.[2] Alfano stressed that China has become a "leading partner" for Italy. If we attempt to paint a (non-exhaustive) picture of Chinese investments in Italy, we can say that Chinese equity holdings in the country are quite considerable. The shares of the People's Bank of China alone, which holds stakes in companies such as Atlantia, Intesa Sanpaolo, UniCredit, Enel and Telecom Italia, are worth a total of 4.395 billion euros, as indicated by *Il Sole 24 Ore* in May of 2017; in 398 Italian companies the stake exceeds 10 percent.[3] According to the CESIF Report for the Italy China Foundation, in 2017 Chinese investors are present in a total of 514 Italian companies, and if we consider only their investments (excluding those from Hong Kong) we find a total of 26,039 employees and a turnover of 13.991 billion euros. Above all, Beijing is also present in Italy in sectors considered as strategic, including in terms of security. Top brands such as Pirelli, Wind Tre or Esaote are not the only ones that speak Mandarin. We cannot forget the stake held in CDP Reti (the holding company that controls critical energy infrastructure, Snam and Terna), or the acquisition of Ansaldo Energia. Nor can we fail to mention the penetration of the market by Chinese companies such as Huawei and ZTE, not only with sales, or the presence in Milan of the rating agency Dagong. Italy is not only a tourist destination, it is a significant entranceway to the Old Continent.

We will return to the evaluations of national security soon. For now let us stick to the numbers and strictly economic prospects. Although there was a drop of 13 percent in the first half of 2018 compared to the same period the previous year, Beijing's investment initiatives are destined to continue in the coming years, although at a level of greater stability.

> The drop in Italy is due to divestment from sectors not considered strategic – explained Marco Marazzi, head of the China Desk of Baker Mckenzie to *il Sole 24 Ore* – in line with the indications of the Chinese government, that last year began to place filters on foreign investment of a speculative nature, especially in sectors such as real estate, soccer or entertainment. [...] There will be a consolidation in the shift to sectors considered more strategic – he specified – such as technology, biomedical or infrastructure. In addition, we will see less M&A and more joint ventures of opening of stores or greenfield investments (opening of branches, -ed.) by mid-size Chinese family enterprises.[4]

So there is a consolidation of operations that are rarely in the news, often because they are carried out by unlisted companies, which are not obliged to provide communications to the market and are often not eager to appear in public. It's the lesson taught by Henry Kissinger. In any event, China does not move randomly, but within a clear strategic framework. Their plan is contained in the cited One Belt One Road program, but also in the Made in China 2015 program, which should not be underestimated. To put it briefly, the idea is to go from being the workshop of the world to being the hotbed of innovation. That is the front on which the global challenge will be won, and that is where Beijing aims, producing both success and worries. We have seen a reaction from US intelligence, that has made explicit accusations against Huawei and ZTE, giants that are very present in Italy despite the fact that the Department for Security Information (Italy's national intelligence service) has warned of the risks of foreign penetration in areas that are particularly sensitive in terms of national security.

When the claws come out …

In Italy, the prospect of increasing business with China has prevailed over considerations relating to security. The true turning point in bilateral relations took place in 2014, when Renzi came to Palazzo Chigi. It was then that the new prime minister, together with Franco Bassanini, at the time the president of the public investment bank Cassa Depositi e Prestiti (CDP), launched one of the most significant, and controversial, financial and industrial operations along the Rome–Beijing axis. At the end of July 2014, with a ceremony at Italian government headquarters, a deal was signed between CDP and State Grid International Development, a Chinese state company considered the top utility in the world (Fortune 500). For slightly more than 2 billion euros, 35 percent of CDP Reti was sold, the vehicle created by Prime Minister Enrico Letta to "protect" critical and strategic infrastructure such as Terna and Snam (Italgas was added later). That company was supposed to allow for a sort of separation of the network from the two main operators, Eni and Enel, and at the same time protect their assets from potential foreign purchases. In 2013, the worry was linked precisely to Chinese aims. With Renzi the paradigm shifted, and the capital of CDP Reti was opened up to the Asian investor. This took place without the activation of the *golden power* procedure due to the absence of the implementation decree, that although it was already ready and available at the government offices, the prime minister only signed later.[5] The sale was intended to go on without a hitch, and it did.

Among the critical voices at the time were the online daily *Formiche* and the Five-Star Movement, which submitted a parliamentary question on the matter. The prime minister had in fact been in Beijing just a few weeks earlier (June 2014), where he also signed a three-year plan of action, meeting numerous economic operators, including the management of State Grid, and promoted agreements such as that between the Ministry of Economic Development and the online retail giant Alibaba. The latter deal was considered one of the most important links between the then-secretary of the PD and Beijing (by way of Marco Carrai, a brilliant entrepreneur and personal friend of Renzi).[6] After that first visit other important missions followed, such as the immediately subsequent trip by Economics Minister Padoan and the visit to Rome of Chinese Prime Minister Li Keqiang. An additional important meeting between Renzi and Xi was held in November of the following year in Sardinia, while the visit by President of the Republic Mattarella to Beijing took place in 2017, sealing a relationship that by that time had become particularly strong. In the meantime there had been not only an increase in trade, but also an intense M&A activity on the part of the Chinese in Italy, in addition to a very significant geopolitical and economic decision by Italy, that of joining the Asian Infrastructure Investment Bank, the principal multilateral bank led by Beijing. It was an epochal act of trust in the Chinese contribution to development. Thus not only had Rome sold both public and private strategic assets, but it had also chosen to directly participate in one of the most important initiatives in the plans for China's growth in influence.

Not just Confucius: the Italian–Chinese connection

In Italy the Dragon can count on a vast network of associations, interest groups and figures of various types who are legitimately involved in the promotion of Sino-Italian friendship. Thus there is more than just the network of Confucius Institutes, that is particularly widespread in our territory. By now an "official" and certainly valuable role is played by the Italy China Foundation, currently chaired by the entrepreneur and former parliamentarian Alberto Bombassei, but created and led for almost 15 years by Cesare Romiti. This foundation has a permanent training school, a study center focused on businesses (the CESIF) and a close connection with two other significant organizations: the Italo-Chinese Chamber of Commerce, chaired by Pier Luigi Streparava, and the Italo-Chinese Institute led by Mario Boselli, Official Ambassador of Shanghai Fashion Week and president of Banca 5, in the Intesa Sanpaolo banking group. In 2014 a new institution was added, the Italy China Cultural Forum, that was strongly desired and coordinated by Francesco Rutelli, former Minister of Culture and a leading representative of the moderate area of the center-left. An older group is the Italy China Association based in Rome, while more recently, the Italy China Project Foundation was founded in Verona, led by Xin Wang and active in particular in relations with Sichuan. There are also associations such as Sviluppo Cina (China Development) in Milan or Sviluppo Italia Cina in Rome. The Italy China Business Forum is also very important, co-chaired by the very authoritative figures Marco Tronchetti Provera of Pirelli on the Italian side and Tian Guoli, president of the Bank of China for the Chinese. The most recent initiative, which is no less important on a political-institutional level, is the Institute for Chinese Culture founded in April 2017 by former PD Senator Alessandro Maran, whose president is Vito Petrocelli, Chairman of the Foreign Affairs Committee of the Senate, and which has a network of "ambassadors" in the Italian regions led by former parliamentarian Roberto Cociancich and an advisory committee chaired by former Education Minister Stefania Giannini. This is a significant instrument in addition to numerous other venues that with different forms and aims work for better relations between the two countries. For example, it is important not to underestimate the strength of the Italian Chinese community, that a 2016 report of the Ministry of Labor quantifies as 300,000 people with regular permits of stay, along with associations of Chinese students in Italian universities (at the Bocconi and Polytechnic of Turin, to cite just two), and the Chinese merchants association or the influential Associna group, that brings together second-generation Chinese.[7]

This extensive network also relies on figures in the world of politics, communication and the economy, who have always represented important links between China and Italy. A prominent position is reserved for the journalist Francesco Scisci, an Italian voice to which both sides listen carefully. He is the one who interviewed Pope Francis for *Asia Times*. A key person for high-level relations is also Franco Bernabè, who for 12 years was on the board of Petro-China, a company with a significant role in the Celestial Empire. A long-term visitor to Chinese venues is Giancarlo Elia Valori, for whose mother Emilia a building of the University of Beijing was named, that houses the faculty of International Relations. A person who has always kept close political ties with China, and still does, is certainly Romano Prodi. Other figures have earned great consideration such as former Ambassador Umberto Vattani, now the president of Venice International University (which has considerable relations with Chinese universities) and former Environment Minister Corrado Clini, member of the advisory board of the influential Chinese organization Global Energy Interconnection Development and Cooperation Organization. On an economic level, we should note Alberto Forchielli, partner and founder of the Mandarin Capital Partners fund and the Asia Observatory, and Luigi Gambardella, a manager first at Telecom Italia and currently at Open Fiber, who founded the lobbying association ChinaEU, and whom the American website *Politico* has called "Europe's Mr. China – Brussels' biggest Beijing booster."[8] Not bad.

Italy is also present on the Silk Road

According to a study carried out by Professor Enrico Fardella of the University of Beijing, the penetration capacity of Chinese soft power in Italy has had particular success thanks to the launch of the Belt and Road Initiative. A survey by the Pew Institute has confirmed, with hard data, that in the period from 2014 to 2017 the perception of China in Italy improved dramatically, with a reduction of unfavorable opinions from 70 to 59 percent. In Fardella's analysis, the figure is explained with the sudden growth of Chinese investments (14 billion euros) carried out by the People's Bank of China (PBOC) in Italian strategic assets (Cassa Depositi e Prestiti, Mediobanca, Generali, Eni, Enel, Telecom, Saipem: all above the threshold of 2 percent that triggers the Consob transparency obligations for significant equity holdings). This financial activism has also been perceived by public opinion as an expression of trust in Italy's economic and financial stability at a time when the economic crisis had seriously weakened the country. The One Belt One Road initiative led to the publication of numerous articles and journalistic reports that improved the perception of China, and the same trend – Fardella notes – can be seen from the reading of parliamentary questions in 2014 and 2015; those that were positive regarding China and encouraged greater involvement and cooperation doubled in 2014, while in 2015 they returned to the 2013 levels.

> The contents of parliamentary questions from 2013 until the end of 2017 confirm the data gathered by the Pew Institute: the vast majority had a negative attitude towards China. All of these, however, are based on economic issues: fake products (15.6%), unfair competition (14.5%), black market (12.3%) and dumping (9%), while it is interesting to see that the only positive ones were linked to the BRI (Italian participation in the AIIB, Chinese investments in Italy, and port infrastructure).

The designs on strategic infrastructure

Not everyone in the country is convinced that the arrival of Chinese investors brings only benefits for Italian companies and the economy as a whole. A careful analysis is contained in the essay *Red Capitalism: Chinese Investments in Italy* by the economist Andrea Goldstein, who does not hide the possibility that there are "geopolitical aims behind Chinese investments in Italy."[9]

> In this historical period, there is above all a desire to somehow crack the alliance between Europe and the United States. Being present in the Italian economy – Goldstein writes – allows Beijing to indirectly influence European processes on specific points on which Rome's voice and vote are important in Brussels.

In his writing he analyzes what happened in 2014:

> It is worrying that, despite the unquestionable strategic value of Snam and Terna for the country, not even the CDP Reti operation raised a debate on the strategic repercussions of such a bold decision. The silence of the Copasir was deafening […] that just a few months earlier had expressed worries about the national security repercussions of the entry of the Spanish into Telecom Italia.

The economist's attention was also gabbed by the decision by ENI to sell 28.75 percent of ENI East Africa to the Chinese of CNPC, a company which controls offshore field 4 in Mozambique, "one of the most promising areas in the entire world."

The fears expressed by Goldstein in his book were subsequently confirmed in a document of May 28, 2018 in which the European Commission expressed an opinion on the state of EU-China relations with the goal of protecting the interests of the member states. Italy, France and Germany the report states, have revealed particular worries regarding the possibility that foreign groups, "including Chinese groups, obtain knowledge and modern technologies at low cost and with unfair methods, thanks to the purchase" of European companies, as reported by the Portuguese press agency Lusa.[10] Thus, various countries in the European Union have stated their willingness to create legislation aimed at regulating these relations, since "in 2017, 68 percent of Chinese investments in Europe came from state enterprises"; the Commission then expressed "worries about the acquisitions orchestrated by the State that could be an obstacle to European strategic interests, public safety goals, competitiveness and employment."[11] In reality, Rome tends to give precedence to business opportunities over security needs. And while Western intelligence services are all occupied with protecting their strategic infrastructure and assisting governments in competition for 5G technology (and in general protecting the telecommunications sector), in Italy we see that the Chinese deputy prime minister visits a large company such as Open Fiber together with the CEO of Huawei and is accompanied with the entire delegation inside the SOC (Security Operation Center), that is, the facility that processes the most sensitive information, which would normally require a particular authorization for access (that would not be possible to give to a foreign delegation). This happened in December 2017, and it was left to the online daily *Formiche.net* to report the case, requesting an intervention by the parliamentary commission on secret services to better understand the implications of the matter.[12] The newspaper *Il Fatto Quotidiano* also took up the question. The deputy director Stefano Feltri wrote:

> Two publicly-controlled companies, Enel and CDP, are shareholders of Open Fiber, the fiber company at the center of government strategy. The State Grid Corporation of China, a Chinese state elephant, is in CDP Reti […].[13] Imagine if Putin's number three official had taken a stroll in the rooms of a strategic company, those that keep the heads of intelligence up at night. There would have been an uproar. But are we sure we should worry less about the Chinese?

Surprise surprise, a few weeks later it was announced that Huawei had won the tender to supply O&M (Operations & Maintenance) monitoring systems for the Open Fiber fiber network. What is important is not the value of the contract (only 10 million euros), but the fact that Chinese technology will manage and control the quality of the optical links of the top ten Italian cities (for now). The Celestial Empire was also successful regarding the *ultra broadband* sector with ZTE's victory in the tender for development of the Wind Tre network. Among other things, ZTE also committed to realizing the 5G networks in Rome, Milan and Turin, with a partnership that also includes Open Fiber (as well as Vodafone and Telecom). Naturally, the socio-employment impact promised is consistent with the company's ambitions, that in 2017–18 had already gone from 60 to 600 professional employees, with the promise at the end of 2016 to invest 900 million euros and hire 2,500 youth in Italy's South. According to the Chinese giant, there will be no negative repercussions from the clash underway with the US Administration. This is in part – we may add – because in Italy there is little consciousness of the reasons why the United States and its institutions are so worried about the commercial and technological aggressiveness of Beijing in sectors that have always been considered sensitive for security.

Red, yellow, green: the continuous link between Rome and Beijing

The shift from the Renzi–Gentiloni governments to the M5S–League government (at times identified by the "political colors" of the two partners: yellow and green, respectively) has not led to a change in approach towards China; quite the contrary. The crisis of confidence that has hit Italy, with a sharp increase in the spread (the difference between yields on Italian and German state bonds) and the tension on the markets regarding our public debt in general, has consolidated the idea of a strengthening of the special relationship with the Dragon. The Economics Minister, Professor Giovanni Tria, has an old and well-structured familiarity with the Chinese, and like his predecessor Pier Carlo Padoan, is counting on a mission to Beijing to allow him to return to Italy with an additional stock of financial oxygen. The rigorous commitment by the minister, along with that of his colleague Paolo Savona (who also knows the Asian giant quite well), does not only have a "technical" value. Deputy Prime Minister

Luigi Di Maio has chosen to create a China task force at the Ministry of Economic Development aimed at "developing a national systemic strategy, aimed at strengthening economic and commercial relations." The government press release stressed the "primary" objective of "strengthening the relations between China and Italy in trade, finance, investments and R&D and cooperation in third countries, allowing Italy to position itself as a preferred partner and leader in Europe in strategic projects such as the Belt and Road Initiative and Made in China 2025."[14] A considerable goal.

The task force is the result of the impetus from Michele Geraci, who will be the coordinator of this control room. The Undersecretary of Economic Development is such a big fan of Xi's regime that the newspaper *Avvenire* dedicated a profile to him. The journalist of the newspaper published by the Italian Bishops Conference wrote: "To hear what he thinks, Geraci seems to be an ambassador of the Chinese government."[15] What follows is in fact a review of the declarations that Geraci, a financial expert who teaches at the University of Zhejiang, gave to a video blog we came across earlier, *Byoblu* run by Claudio Messora of M5S. Geraci also expressed his ideas on China on Beppe Grillo's blog in April and then June 2018. In his view, the Dragon can resolve any of Italy's problems, from the purchase of state bonds to an environmental transformation, passing through a tutorship on immigration and public order.[16] And Italy should offer Beijing the strategic assets represented by the port of Trieste, explains Geraci, who in a later interview with *Formiche.net* added that he does not want "to sell off the country's strategic assets."[17]

Trieste would undoubtedly be a coup for the New Silk Road. But what about Italy's interests and the more general framework of our international alliances? The economic perspective seems to prevail entirely over any strategic considerations. It may be that the horse has already bolted. As in the game of weiki, China has taken steps that are not so short, but are absolutely decisive. On the other hand, Italy, unlike other European countries, that are moving rapidly to make amends, does not have an instrument to verify and potentially block the entry of foreign capital into the country's economy. In the US there is the CFIUS (Committee on Foreign Investment in the United States), Italy only has the golden power; a dam that may not be sufficient to stop another type of power, sharp power.

Notes

[1] H. Kissinger, *Cina*, Milan, Mondadori, 2011.
[2] Italy China Foundation, "Rapporto annuale 2017, presentazione a Roma," 18/7/2017, www.italychina.org. On the Italy China's website highlights are available of the Foundation's annual report, *Cina 2017. Scenari e prospettive per le imprese*.
[3] A. Franceschi, "Chi sono e che cosa comprano i grandi investitori cinesi in Europa," *Il Sole 24 Ore*, 4/5/2017, www.ilsole24ore.com.
[4] G. Mancini, "Meno calcio e più hi-tech: Il nuovo corso degli investimenti cinesi in Italia," *Il Sole 24 Ore*, 19/8/2018, www.ilsole24ore.com.
[5] The golden power is an option that allows governments to intervene in the activities of companies that operate in strategic sectors (such as energy, defense and national security), for example voting in advance an acquisition of such a company.
[6] One of the most important European managers for Alibaba, Mattia Mor, was elected to Parliament in 2018 as a candidate with the Democratic Party.
[7] Ministry of Labor and Social Policies, *La comunità cinese in Italia. Rapporto annuale sulla presenza dei migranti*, 2016, www.integrazionemigranti.gov.it.
[8] N. Hirst, "Europe's Mr. China," *Politico*, 31/5/2017, www.politico.com.
[9] A. Goldstein, *Capitalismo rosso: Gli investimenti cinesi in Italia*, Milan, Università Bocconi Editore, 2016.
[10] European Parliament, Committee on International Trade, *Opinion of the Committee on International Trade Addressed to the Committee for Foreign Affairs on the State of EU–China Relations (2017/2274(INI))*, Rapporteur for Opinion: Iuliu Winkler, 29/5/2018, http://www.europarl.europa.eu.
[11] R. Baptista, "Investimenti cinesi in Italia tra sfide, opportunità e iniziative," *Inside Marketing*, 6/7/2018, www.insidemarketing.it.
[12] P. Di Michele, "Chi si preoccupa (e perché) della presenza economica della Cina in Italia," *Formiche.net*, 13/12/2017, www.formiche.net.
[13] S. Feltri, "Capitani di sventura. Ombre cinesi che devono preoccuparci," *Il Fatto Quotidiano*, 13/12/2017.
[14] Ministry of Economic Development, "Il MISE lancia la Task Force Cina," 20/8/2018, http://sviluppoeconomico.gov.it.
[15] P. Saccò, "Michele Geraci, un fan di Xi al ministero dello Sviluppo economico," *Avvenire*, 22/8/2018, www.avvenire.it.
[16] M. Geraci, "La Cina e il governo del cambiamento," *Il Blog di Beppe Grillo*, 11/6/2018, www.beppegrillo.it.
[17] F. Bechis, "Così ci apriamo alla Cina ma senza svendere asset strategici," *Formiche.net*, 3/9/2018, www.formiche.net. See also D. Taino, "Al centro dell'Europa: Ecco perché ai cinesi piace il porto di Trieste," *Corriere della Sera*, 19/8/2018, www.corriere.it.

Conclusions

Warning: in dealing with a complex and "new" question like sharp power, it is easy to make two mistakes, that are equal and opposite. There is the attempt to feed what is defined as a phobia centered from time to time on Russia, China or Iran. On the other hand, the opposite risk is to ignore the threat believing it is a stratagem, perhaps a form of interference originating from the United States. In reality, as we have attempted to demonstrate in the preceding pages, the phenomenon of sharp power exists and must be taken into due consideration. The challenge presented to our society and our democracies is the responsibility of everyone, and of policymakers in particular. Although we cannot reach definitive conclusions, we can try to put in order some considerations, or suggestions.

How do we combat the war of information and the increasingly massive use of "sharp" instruments of influence? What countermeasures are most effective? These are questions that do not have a single, definitive answer. What is certain is that we cannot face these challenges alone. The threat regards single countries but also Western democracy more in general. This is why it makes sense to count on international cooperation, especially in the Atlantic area, and not have the illusion of being able to resolve everything in an autarchic dimension. If in Europe, and in Italy, the awareness of sharp power has only been developed very recently, in the United States – as we have seen – the analysis is in a more advanced phase. That makes it natural to follow the debate there.

An interesting response has come from three brilliant young researchers: Alina Polyakova, David M. Rubenstein Fellow at the Brookings Institution, and Geysha Gonzalez, Associate Director of the Eurasia Center at the Atlantic Council. In the pages of the *Washington Post* they presented a concept that is bold in a certain sense, but definitely effective.[1] They traced a parallel between foreign interference and the anti-smoking campaign fought by US authorities starting in 1964. The experts ask: what allowed the success of that campaign, that was able to halve the number of smokers and prohibit smoking in public establishments? "Much like Big Tobacco in the 1950s, the tech industry today operates in an unregulated environment. Facebook, Twitter and Google are all keen to avoid being treated as media companies, which would make them subject to a slew of Federal Communications Commission regulations." To date the corrective actions these giants have prepared on their platforms "are failing to curtail the spread of disinformation, and sooner or later the tech industry will have to face the same FCC restrictions on content and advertising as traditional media." In addition, to carry out effective campaigns, the message to be transmitted is not the only thing that counts; who transmits it is essential. Part of the success of the anti-smoking campaign is in fact due to the report that established a clear connection between smoking and cancer, published in 1964 by the office of the Surgeon General of the United States, an indisputably authoritative source. "Research shows," note Polyakova and Gonzalez, "that even truthful information will be dismissed by audiences if it doesn't come from a trusted source."

A third point that the researchers consider essential to combat foreign interference and disinformation regards the involvement of the private sector. Again referring to the US government campaign against smoking, they recall that organizations of civil society were the ones that produced television, radio or newspaper advertisements that described the negative effects of smoking, and pushed for smoking to be banned in public areas. Likewise, it is necessary now for governments to act to fund independent initiatives that are useful for the purpose, and for private organizations and tech companies to allocate greater resources for projects that can enhance awareness in public opinion. A serious campaign of civic education is needed for the digital era. "Just as we teach children about the health risks associated with smoking, we should also educate them to become critical consumers of information," the two US researchers write. This is a challenge that applies on both sides of the Atlantic.

Culture, culture, culture; there is no doubt about what is needed. Yet we cannot ignore the fact that when we address the issue of sharp power and international relations, we inevitably end up discussing national security and the strategic interests of a country, a community or an alliance. This is why the push to increase awareness in the population cannot but be accompanied by actions that more properly come under the competence of states. Sharing of information, security, transparency and investments in research and development on artificial intelligence (AI) and computational propaganda; these are the areas in which it is necessary to intervene more decisively, and urgently. As we have seen in this book, the playing field of sharp power is the infosphere, cybernetic space. This is the space that must be monitored.

The battle plays out on the frontier of innovation. If on the one hand the existing instruments and methods to target Western interests will be gradually identified and neutralized, on the other, technology will continue to progress, it will become financially more accessible, and malicious actors will continue to evolve their tactics. This is why is it essential not to limit oneself to a reactive approach, that simply aims to fill the gaps of existing vulnerabilities or respond on a case-by-case basis. Single countries, like Italy, cannot do it themselves. The need to develop a collaborative strategy on a transatlantic level cannot be deferred.

Suggestions in this direction are offered by a study produced by the Brookings Institution, an American think tank, that proposes three lines of action.[2] The first regards precisely the sharing of information. European governments, the United States and its allies, must set up information exchange mechanisms with companies in the private sector. Technological companies should voluntarily cooperate with public sector agencies, in particular with the intelligence community, to establish a rapid alarm system when disinformation activities are detected in their systems. To that end, the experts write, it would make sense for national governments, the European Union and NATO to establish a designated interlocutor within the intelligence agencies that can be the point of contact to receive and distribute that information, depending on the specific situations. A voluntary system of information sharing would be ideal, but the authors stress that such processes could also be required by law. NATO, as the principal defense and security organization that keeps the transatlantic partnership together, could take on a leading role in the coordination and sharing of information through existing and new mechanisms in the context of the Alliance's Cyber Command or the Joint Intelligence and Security (JIS) Division. Lastly, it would be good for European governments and the US to regularly convene the StratCom, Hybrid Threat and Cyber Threat task forces that currently exist within the various agencies. An annual

StratCom forum should be instituted in Brussels with the participation of the United States and its European allies.

The second point regards the improvement of security and transparency of information. The EU and the USA, the report argues, should order an immediate check of government information systems, and the security of classified networks and systems. That review should have the aim of identifying current vulnerabilities and at the same time identifying emerging threats. In turn, social media companies should have the obligation to develop instruments to rapidly identify fake and automated accounts (known as bots). The media should pay greater attention to preventing malicious actors from promoting their content (perhaps banning them or pushing their material lower in search engines). Tech giants could accept codes of conduct regarding advertising and the use of personal data, favor transparency in the flows of advertising proceeds and extend restrictions on political advertising already in place for traditional media, to online spaces. Lastly, the academic institutions that are responsible for educating the next generation of IT experts should introduce ethics courses, because ultimately, algorithms are written by human beings, and thus they have intrinsic prejudices incorporated in them, and are anything but "neutral" (greater awareness of this fact could make algorithms and AI less susceptible to manipulation).

A final plan of action regards the need to invest strategically in research and development. The new frontiers that will determine the balance of power in the future are AI and computational propaganda. Governments, private foundations, non-profit organizations and technology companies must work together with the academic world, including to better understand how technological progress will influence public matters. Although it is indisputable that AI will positively transform many sectors – health, transportation and others – it is just as important to study and recognize the negative potential and "political" implications of new technologies. Investment is needed, for example, in research that examines not just the "supply side" but also the "demand side" of disinformation linked to foreign interference. The typical narratives of a certain sharp power are spread because individuals find them attractive. Techniques and instruments are only part of the equation. Better understanding of the social psychology of online disinformation would help governments, independent media and civil society groups to be better equipped to combat that propaganda.

The work to be carried out is considerable, and involves a great number of actors and disciplines. Understanding the dynamics of sharp power and developing an adequate capacity for resilience becomes essential to protect Western democracies and values from the global competition that technological disruption has made less soft than we imagine.

Notes

[1] A. Polyakova, G. Gonzalez, "The US anti-smoking campaign is a great model for fighting disinformation," *The Washington Post*, 4/8/2018, www.washingtonpost.com.

[2] A. Polyakova, S. Boyer, *The Future of Political Warfare: Russia, the West, and the Coming Age of Global Digital Competition*, Brookings – Robert Bosch Foundation Transatlantic Initiative, 3.2018, www.brookings.edu.

Acknowledgments

This book would never have seen the light of day without the determination of the publisher and in particular of Orsola Matrisciano, who from the beginning believed in the importance of trying to discuss this facet of power, that to date has been analyzed little. To her and all of the staff at the publishing company I express my gratitude for the trust placed in me.

A special thanks goes to the editorial staff of *Formiche*, *Cyber Affairs* and *Airpress*. Those are the publications of the small group that I founded and that every day does work which makes me very proud. From the directors Michele Pierri, Flavia Giacobbe and Valeria Covato to valued collaborators such as Emanuele Rossi and Marco Andrea Ciaccia, what is written in this book can be considered a synthesis of a collective, daily analysis, that is published in particular on Formiche (and will continue to be so in the future). Francesco Bechis deserves a mention ad hoc. He is the youngest of all of the associates, but also the person who worked the most on defining the outline and contents of this work, having had the possibility to interview not only Steven Bannon but also figures such as General John Allen, the president of the Brookings Institution, whom I thank for his excellent collaboration.

I wish to recall expert contributions from Professors Giulio Sapelli and Enrico Fardella. It is harder to find the words to express my gratitude to Gianni De Gennaro, who in addition to guiding me in directing the American Studies Center, represents an essential point of reference for me more in general. Lastly, support that was no less important, and not merely formal, came and comes from my family, that in supporting me, and also putting up with me, proved to be an excellent case of *hard power*...

Index of names

AdLabs, 89
Adnow, 89
Advanced Persistent Threat (APT37), 63
Afrobarometer, 17
Agence France-Presse, 41
Ahmadinejad, Mahmoud, 4, 74
Al Arabiya, 18, 49
Al Jazeera, 16, 18, 41, 49
Al Maktoum, Mohammed Bin Rashid, 12
Al Thani, Al Mayassa, 15
Al Thani, Hamad bin Khalifa, 18
Alessandrello, Rosario, 81
Alexander the Great, 8
Alfano, Angelino, 103
Alibaba, 107
al-Jubeir, Adel, 76
All Russia State Television, 44
Allen, John, 62
Alli, Paolo, 48
Alliance Française, 35
Alto Analytics, 83
Amnesty International, 14
Andreotti, Giulio, 90
Annunziata, Lucia, 80
Ansaldo Energia, 104
Antidiplomatico, L', 86, 89
APT33, 72
Arden, Warwick, 21

Argentina, 25
Armenia, 43, 54
Asia Observatory, 108
Asia Times, 107
Asian Infrastructure Investment Bank, 4, 106
Assange, Julian, 61
Assicurazioni Generali, 108
Assicurazioni Generali Russia, 82
Association of Young Italian-Russians (RIM), 80, 81
Associna, 107
Atlantia, 104
Atlantic Council, 47, 115
Australia, 27, 36, 40
Avvenire, 112
Azerbaijan, 5, 43, 54

Baker McKenzie, Banca, 104
Banca 5, 107
Barstow, David, 24
Bassanini, Franco, 105
Belarus, 43
Belgium, 49
Berlusconi, Silvio, 83, 90
Bernabè, Franco, 107
Biden, Joe, 98, 99
Bloomberg, 21, 30
Bocconi University, 107
Bombassei, Alberto, 106

Bonini, Carlo, 89
Boselli, Mario, 107
British Broadcasting Corporation
   (BBC), 8, 16, 18, 41
British Council, 35
British Empire, 9
Brookie, Graham, 100
Brookings Institution, 62, 115, 117
Bush, George W., 24, 62, 90
BuzzFeed News, 67, 86-88
Byoblu, 86, 112

Cable News Network (CNN), 16, 18,
   41, 46, 83
Callegari, Giorgio, 82
Calleo, David, 8
Cambodia, 52
Cameron, David, 9, 90
Campo Russo, 81
Cardin, Ben, 99
Carpenter, Michael, 98, 99
Carrai, Marco, 106
Casaleggio, Davide, 86
Cassa Depositi e Prestiti (CDP), 105,
   108, 110
Catena Umana, 86
CDP Reti, 104, 105, 109, 110
Center for Development
   of Italy- Russia Relations, 82
Center on Public Diplomacy –
   University of Southern California, 12
Central Department of Propaganda –
   Cina, 17
Centre Pompidou, 14
CESIF, 104, 107
Chamaleon, 87
Changchun, Li, 37
Chen, Adrian, 97
Chiesa, Giulietto, 87
China (People's Republic of China), 1,
   3-5, 9-13, 15-18, 21-24, 26, 27, 29-32,
   35-43, 49, 51, 52, 55, 62, 63, 68-70,
   72, 73, 76, 103-112, 115

China Central Television (CCTV), 17,
   41, 42
China Daily, 17
China National Radio, 17, 42
China Radio International, 17, 42
ChinaEU, 108
China-Pakistan Economic Corridor
   (CPEC), 52
Chinese Ocean Shipping Company
   (COSCO), 31
Chinese People's Consultative
   Congress (CPPCC), 27
Chissano, Joaquim, 8
Christian Democracy, 90
Civic Chamber Russia, 47
Clickio, 89
Clini, Corrado, 108
Clinton, Bill, 70
Clinton, Hillary, 47, 67, 68
CNPC, 109
Cociancich, Roberto, 107
Colono Frascati, Giancarlo, 86
Columbia University, 10, 36
Committee on Foreign Investment in
   the United States (CFIUS), 112
Commonwealth, 9
Communist Party of China (CPC), 3,
   4, 11, 12, 16, 17, 27, 36, 37, 41
Communist Party of the Soviet Union
   (CPSU), 2
Confindustria, 82
Confucius, 4, 35, 106
Confucius Institute, 4, 21, 22, 27, 35-
   40, 50, 106
Congress - USA, 52, 74, 99
Connecticut, 18
Conoscere Eurasia, 82
Consob, 106
Conte, Giuseppe, 91, 95, 97, 103
Copasir, 99, 100, 109
Cosa, La, 86
Cozy Bear, 67, 68
Craxi, Bettino, 90

Index of names

Crimea, 3, 5, 46, 64, 66, 79, 95
Criteo, 89
CrowdStrike, 67, 72
Cyber Threat, 117
Cyprus, 92
Czechoslovakia, 5

d'Amico, Claudio, 92
Dagong, 104
Darius III, 8
Democratic National Committee (DNC), 67
Department for Security Information, 105
Department of Defense USA, 24
Department of Justice USA, 48
DFRLab, 47
Dhlakama, Afonso, 8
Di Battista, Alessandro, 95
Di Maio, Luigi, 88, 112
Di Stefano, Manlio, 95
Direttanews, 89
Direttanews24, 86
Djibouti, 52
Doha Tribeca Film Festival, 15
Donbas, 65, 81
Dugin, Alexander, 3, 93

East Germany, 2
Economist, The, 26
Eisenberg, Lewis, 99
Enel, 104, 105, 108, 110
England, 92
Eni, 82, 105, 108, 109
Esaote, 104
Estonia, 43, 64, 65
Eurasia Group, 22
Eurasian Economic Union (EEU), 54
European Commission, 27, 90, 110
European Council, 58, 91
European Council on Foreign Relations (ECFR), 28
European Popular Party, 97
European Union, 10, 27, 54, 58, 110, 117

Facebook, 47, 86, 96, 100, 116
Fallico, Antonio, 82
Fancy Bear, 63, 67, 68
Fardella, Enrico, 108
Fattaccio, Il, 86
Fatto Quotidiano, Il, 92, 110
Federal Bureau of Investigation (FBI), 46, 48, 68, 75, 96
Federal Communications Commission – USA, 24, 116
Federal Office for Protection of the Constitution (BfV) Germany, 30
Federal Security Service of the Russian Federation (FSB), 64
Federalimentare, 82
Feltri, Stefano, 110
Ferlenghi, Ernesto, 82
Financial Times, 29
Finland, 92
FireEye, 47, 67
First Russian TV, 44
Five Star Movement (M5S), 84, 86, 88, 90, 91, 95, 97, 99, 106, 111, 112
FiveThirtyEight, 100
Flying Kitten, 74
Foglio, Il, 94
Forchielli, Alberto, 108
Foreign Affairs, 19, 26, 98
Foreign Affairs Committee, Italian Senate, 95, 107
Foreign Policy, 1
Forensic Research Lab, 100

Formiche, 26, 47, 62, 98, 106, 110, 112
Foschini, Giuliano, 89
France, 23, 49, 91-93, 110
Francis I, Pope, 83, 107
Fucina, La, 86
Fujian, 3, 42
Fukuyama, Francis, 1

Gambardella, Luigi, 108
Gazprom, 54

Gehry, Frank, 13
General Assembly - UN, 69
Gentiloni, Paolo, 91, 111
Georgia, 43, 54, 65
Geraci, Michele, 112
Gerasimov, Valery, 29, 64
Germany, 8, 15, 16, 23, 29, 30, 54, 91, 110
Giannini, Stefania, 107
Giles, Keir, 64
GIM-Unimpresa, 82
Global Energy Interconnection Development and Cooperation Organization - Cina, 108
Global Times, 27, 42
Goethe Institut, 35
Goldstein, Andrea, 109, 110
Gonzalez, Geysha, 115, 116
Google, 86-88, 116
Gorbachev, Mikhail, 2, 7
Government Accountability Office USA, 24
Greece, 31, 52
Grillo, Beppe, 84, 88, 112
Guardian, 49
Guoli, Tian, 107
Guoqing, Wang, 27
Gyatso, Tenzin - Dalai Lama, 21, 38

Halper, Stefan A., 48
Hanban, 35-37, 39, 40, 50
Harris, Harry, 52
Harvard University, 1, 7, 11, 13, 26
Hernández Creus, Xavier (Xavi), 15
Hezbollah, 64
Hispan Tv, 50
Hong Kong, 38, 104
Huawei, 104, 105, 110, 111
Human Rights Watch, 14
Hungary, 92
Hybrid Threat, 117

ICTV, 81
ImolaOggi, 86

In mezz'ora, 80
India, 19, 21, 32, 52
Indonesia, 52
iNews24, 86
Infoa5Stelle, 86
Institute for Chinese Culture, 107
Institute of International Education, 11
Instituto Cervantes, 35
Intellettuale Dissidente, L', 86
Iraq, 2, 24, 53, 75
IRNA (Iranian state news agency), 50
iSIGHT Partners, 66
Islamic Republic of Iran Broadcasting (IRIB), 49, 50
Islamic Revolutionary Guard Corps (IRGC), 50
Islamic State of Iraq and Syria (ISIS), 46
Israel, 5, 53, 61, 64, 73-76
Italgas, 105
Italian Bishops Conference, 112
Italian Communist Party (PCI), 90
Italo-Chinese Institute, 107
Italy, 4, 6, 8, 15, 36, 79-85, 88, 90-93, 95-101, 103-113, 115, 117
Italy China Association, 107
Italy China Business Forum, 107
Italy China Chamber of Commerce, 107
Italy China Cultural Forum, 107
Italy China Foundation, 104, 106
Italy China Project Foundation, 107
Italy-Russia Chamber of Commerce (CCIR), 81, 82
Izz ad-Din al-Qassam Cyber Fighters, 75

Jammu, 32, 52
Jinping, Xi, 3, 5, 11, 12, 21, 35, 40, 42, 52, 69-70
Jintao, Hu, 4, 12, 16, 35, 40, 41, 52
Joint Comprehensive Plan of Action, 4, 76

Joint Intelligence and Security (JIS)
   Division NATO, 117

Kang, Lu, 30
Kashmir, 32, 52
Kazakhstan, 43
Kennedy, Paul, 1, 8
Kenya, 17
Keqiang Li, 70, 106
Khamenei, Ali, 4, 5, 50, 74, 75
King, Julian, 27
Kissinger, Henry, 103, 105
Komitet Gosudarstvennoj Bezopasnosti
   (KGB), 2, 10, 79, 83, 95
Komov, Alexej, 92
Komov, Viktor, 92
Kornilkova, Ekaterina, 81
Kreko, Peter, 79
Kremlin, 3, 27-29, 44, 48, 55, 63-66, 68,
   81-83, 85, 86, 91-96, 98, 99, 101, 103
Kurlantzick, Joshua, 37
Kuwait, 53
Kuznetsov, Vladimir, 48
Kyrgyzstan, 43

Lang, Qiao, 69
Latvia, 43
Lavrov, Sergey 3, 45
Lazarus, 62
Le Pen, Marine, 93
League, 80-82, 84, 85, 88, 90-95, 97-99,
   111
Lebanon, 2, 75
Letta, Enrico, 90, 105
Li, Bailian, 21
Liberia, 17
Libero, 82
Lithuania, 43
Lombardia Russia, 82, 92, 94
Lombardy Region, 82
London School of Economics, 36
Louisiana, 46
Ludwig, Jessica, 23, 25, 39

Lusa, 110
Luttwak, Edward, 61, 63, 72

Macau, 38
Macedonia, 31
Macron, Emmanuel, 10, 14, 84
Main Intelligence Directorate (GRU)
   Russia, 64, 68, 96
Mali, 17
Malinovsky, Vladimir, 25
Malkevich, Alexander, 47
Manchuria, 3
Mandarin Capital Partners, 108
Mandiant, 72
Manenti, Alberto, 99
Maran, Alessandro, 107
Marazzi, Marco, 104
Maroni, Roberto, 82, 92
Marshall Plan, 8
Mastrolilli, Paolo, 97-99
Mattarella, Sergio, 86, 106
Mediobanca, 108
Merkel, Angela, 10, 16, 30, 55, 90
Mesopotamia, 8
Messa, Paolo, 5
Messaggero, Il, 82
Messora, Claudio, 86, 112
Mignogna, Marco, 86
Mille Patrie, 81
Ming, Yao, 16
Minister of Economics Italy, 97
Ministry of Culture (China), 35, 37
Ministry of Economic Development
   Italy, 106, 112
Ministry of Foreign Affairs Italy, 8
Ministry of Foreign Affairs Russia, 44, 80
Ministry of Labor Italy, 107
Moavero Milanesi, Enzo, 95
Moldova, 43
Mongolia, 14
Morisi, Luca, 88
Mozambique, 8, 36, 109
Mueller, Robert, 46, 68, 96, 99

Myanmar, 52

National Endowment for Democracy
  (NED), 5, 23, 25, 27, 29, 32, 39
National People's Congress China, 42
National Security Agency (NSA), 62, 71
National Security Council, 94, 101
National Security Study Group, 61
Nemo, 80
New York Times, 24, 46, 48, 86-88, 97
Newsweek, 11
Niemeyer Center, 14
Niger, 17
Noi con Salvini, 88
North Atlantic Treaty Organization
  (NATO), 2, 28, 29, 48, 49, 55, 58, 64,
  65, 67, 90, 99, 117
North Carolina, 21, 22
North Korea, 61, 63
Nye, Joseph, 2, 5, 7-9, 12, 13, 19, 22, 24,
  26, 79

Obama, Barack, 4, 50, 62, 74, 90, 97, 98
OilRig, 76
Olympic Games, 15, 16, 90
One Belt One Road (OBOR), 4, 30,
  32, 52, 105, 108
Open Fiber, 108, 110, 111
Opinione-Pubblica, 86
Organization of the Petroleum
  Exporting Countries (OPEC), 53
Osipov, Oleg, 80
Osipova, Irina, 81

Padania, la, 82, 86, 92
Padoan, Pier Carlo, 106, 111
Pakistan, 52
Palazzo Chigi, 90, 91, 105
Pandora.tv, 87
Pansa, Alessandro, 100
Parenti, Mario, 99
Parliament - Sweden, 67
Parliament - Ukraine, 48

Parliamentary Assembly – NATO, 28, 48
Parubiy, Andriy, 48
Pentagon, 24, 58, 61, 68, 72, 98
People's Bank of China (PBOC), 104,
  108
People's Daily, 27, 42
People's Liberation Army (PLA), 68, 72
Persia, 8
Peru, 25
Petrocelli, Vito, 95, 107
Petro-China, 10
Pew Research Center, 19
Pirelli, 104, 107
Poland, 25
Political Office of the Communist
  Party (Politburo), 11, 37-39, 70
Politico, 108
Polyakova, Alina, 115, 116
Polytechnic of Turin, 107
Populista, Il, 86
Poroshenko, Petro, 54, 66
Press Tv, 50
Prigozhin, Yevgeny, 46
Primakov, Yevgeny, 3
Prodi, Romano, 90, 108
Prussia, 8
Public Prosecutor's Office, 96
Pulitzer, 24
Putin, Vladimir, 2, 3, 5, 25, 43, 46, 49, 54,
  64, 79-84, 86-88, 90-93, 97, 99, 110

Qatar, 2, 14-16, 18, 49, 53
Qatar Foundation, 15
Qatar Investment Authority, 15
Qatar Museums (QM) Authority, 15
Qatar Sports Investments, 15
Qichen, Qian, 11

Radio Broadcasting Company
  (VGTRK), 44
Radio Free Europe, 17
Radio Liberty, 17
Rai 2, 80

Index of names

Rai 3, 80
Rasmussen, Anders Fogh, 99
Razov, Sergey, 80, 94, 95
Reagan, Ronald, 5, 25
Red Hacker Alliance, 72
Renzi, Matteo, 87, 88, 90, 91, 97, 103, 105, 106, 111
Reporters Without Borders (RWB), 43
Repubblica, la, 89
repubblica24.com, 86
Revolutionary Guard - Iran, 75, 76
Ria Fan, 47
Ria Novosti, 83
Rocket Kitten, 76
Romiti, Cesare, 106
Rosneft, 54, 83
Rossotrudnichestvo, 80-82
Rouhani, Hassan, 4, 5, 50, 73, 75, 76
Rousseau Association, 86
Rubenstein Fellowship, David M., 115
Rubio, Marco, 26
Russia (Russian Federation), 1-3, 5, 6, 8, 22-26, 28, 29, 32, 40, 43, 44, 46-49, 51, 54, 55, 62-66, 69, 72, 73, 76, 80-85, 88-100, 115
Russia Today (RT), 43, 44, 83
Rutelli, Francesco, 107

Saipem, 108
Salvini, Matteo, 80-82, 84, 85, 88, 91-95
Sandworm, 66
Sant'Egidio Community, 8
Santiago del Cile, 37
Sapelli, Giulio, 40
Saudi Arabia, 5, 53, 74-76
Savoini, Gianluca, 82, 92, 94
Savona, Paolo, 97, 111
Schmitt, Carl, 3
Scisci, Francesco, 107
Scordamaglia, Luigi Pio, 82
Sechin, Igor, 83
Security Operation Center (SOC), 110
Senate - USA, 27, 48
Serbia, 92
Shadow Brokers, The, 62
Shambaugh, David, 39
Shanghai Cooperation Organization (SCO), 69
Sichuan, 107
Skripal, 48, 91
skytg24news, 86
Slovakia, 25
Small Leading Group for Internet Security and Informatization, 70
Snam, 104, 105, 109
Sole 24 Ore, Il, 104
Sorinet Group, 74
Soros, George, 85
South Ossetia, 65
Sovranità, 81
Spain, 92
Spengler, Oswald, 8
Springer Nature, 29
Sputnik, 43, 44, 49, 82, 84, 85, 87, 92, 98, 101
Sri Lanka, 52
Stamos, Alex, 100
Stampa, La, 97-100
StarTimes, 17
State Council of Information Office (SCIO) China, 38, 70
State Grid Corporation of China, 110
State Grid International Development, 105
State Network and Information Security Coordination Small Group, 70
Stolyarov, Alexei, 48
StratCom, 117
Strategic Support Force (SSF) – China, 71
Streparava, Pier Luigi, 107
Sviluppo Cina, 107
Sviluppo Italia Cina, 107
Sweden, 67
Switzerland, 92
Syria, 2, 8, 75

Taiwan, 29, 38, 70
Talebano, Il, 86
Tass, 80
Tecnimont, 81
Telecom Italia, 104, 108, 109, 111
Terna, 104, 105, 109
tgcom24news, 86
Third Department (3/PLA) - Cina, 71
Tibet, 29, 38
Todaro, Vincenzo, 86
Tourism Development and In-vestment Company (TDIC), 14
Tria, Giovanni, 111
Tronchetti Provera, Marco, 107
Trump, Donald, 1, 4, 10, 48, 50, 51, 55, 72, 76, 79, 99
Turkmenistan, 43
Twitter, 13, 45, 46, 96, 99, 100, 116
TzeTze, 86, 87

Ukraine, 3, 43, 54, 66, 79, 91, 95
UniCredit, 104
Union of Soviet Socialist Republics (USSR), 10, 11
Unit 61398, 71
Unit 61486, 71
United Arab Emirates, 12, 14, 49, 53, 74
United Kingdom, 8, 36, 49, 91
United Nations (UN), 2, 31, 69
United Russia, 92, 93, 99
United States of America (USA), 1, 2, 4, 7, 9, 11, 13, 16, 17, 23, 26, 29, 36, 37, 40, 47, 49-51, 55, 62, 64, 69, 70, 72-76, 79-81, 83, 85, 90, 91, 95-98, 109, 111, 112, 115-118
United States Pacific Command (USPACOM), 52
University of Beijing, 108
University of Michigan, 11
University of North Carolina, 21
University of Zhejiang, 112
USA Really. Wake Up Americans, 47

Uzbekistan, 43

Valori, Giancarlo Elia, 108
Van Herpen, Marcel H., 79
Vattani, Umberto, 108
Venice International University, 108
Vietnam, 64, 70
Virginia, 9
Visegrad Group, 3
VKontakte, 45
Voci dalla Strada, 86
Voice of America (VOA), 17, 41
VoxNews, 94

Walker, Cristopher, 23, 25, 39
Walt, Stephen, 1
Wang, Xin, 107
Washington Post, 94, 95, 115
Web365, 86
Weymouth, Lally, 94
White House, 4, 10, 48, 50, 62, 68, 101
Wikileaks, 59
Wind Tre, 104, 111
World Cup, soccer, 15, 16, 91
World Trade Organization (WTO), 2, 51

Xiangsui, Wang, 69
Xiaoping, Deng, 3
Xinhua, 27
Xinhua News Service, 42

Yanukovych, Viktor, 54
Yeltsin, Boris, 2
Yemen, 2, 75
Yi, Wang, 30

Zanjani, Babak, 75
Zedong, Mao, 3, 4, 35, 40, 103
Zemin, Jiang, 41, 70
Zheleznyak, Sergey 93, 99
ZTE, 104, 105, 111